Oracle Certification Prep

Study Guide for

1Z0-053: Oracle Database 11g:

Administration II

Matthew Morris

Study Guide for Oracle Database 11g: Administration II (Exam 1Z0-053) Rev 1.0

ISBN-13: 978-1482090000
ISBN-10: 1482090007

Table of Contents

What to Expect from the Test

The test consists of 78 multiple choice and multiple answer questions and you will have 120 minutes to complete it. The passing score listed on Oracle Education at this time is 66%, but as with all Oracle certification tests, they note it is subject to change. For multiple-answer questions, you must provide all of the correct answers to get credit for the question. All questions are weighted evenly, so you must get 52 or more correct in order to pass the exam. Answer every question – an unanswered question counts off the same amount as an incorrect one. Take your time reading the question and all of the answers. Sometimes later questions will answer earlier ones and I have found that marking questions I'm not sure of and re-reading them again at the end of the test is valuable.

The first exam in the Database Administrator track, 1Z0-052 is intended to determine whether the person taking it is aware of the basics of the Oracle database architecture and administration. Passing that test does not ensure that the individual can work as a database administrator on their own. The largest single focus of 1Z0-053 is to ensure that an individual who passes the test understands the rudiments of the single most important task of database administration. Protect the data! There are seventy-two distinct objectives listed by Oracle Education for this exam. Of those seventy-two, forty-seven topics are directly or indirectly related to backing up or recovering data. That is 65% of the test. Thirty-nine of those (54% of the exam) are topics directly related to RMAN. If you are not familiar with using RMAN, you are extremely unlikely to pass this exam. If you were going to pick just one book to read other than this guide (and I highly suggest you do more than that), it would have to be Oracle's RMAN User Guide.

The remaining objectives of the exam, such as ASM, tuning, resource management, and the Scheduler are all important topics for a DBA to be knowledgeable of. However the problems of a badly-tuned database that makes sub-optimal use of resources and requires a lot of manual intervention (that should have been automated with Scheduler) pale to insignificance beside a database that cannot be started due to corruption in the SYSTEM tablespace... and for which no backups exist.

Study all of the objectives for this exam, but work doubly hard on ensuring that you understand how to use RMAN. That knowledge will help you on the test and it will be critical if you are ever in charge of administrating an Oracle database.

What to Expect from this Study Guide

This book is built around the subject matter topics that Oracle Education has indicated will be tested. I've gathered together material from several Oracle documentation sources along with examples and illustrations to familiarize you with the types of questions you're likely to see on the test. The guide covers a significant percentage of the information and operations that you must be familiar with in order to pass.

What this guide is intended to do is to present the information that will be covered on the exam at the level it will likely be asked. The guide assumes that you have passed 1Z0-052 and therefore have a reasonable level of knowledge of the Oracle database. No book in and of itself is a substitute for hands-on experience. In preparing for this exam, you should install and configure an Oracle database, create users and tables, and use RMAN to create backups and perform restore operations. Practicing the concepts discussed on this guide on your own database prior to scheduling your exam will improve your probability of success greatly. Since Oracle has made the Oracle XE version of its database free to download and use, there is no reason why anyone who wants to learn to use Oracle cannot get hands-on experience.

The goal of this guide is to present to you the concepts and information most likely to be the subject of test questions, and to do so in a very compact format that will allow you to read through it more than once to reinforce the information. If much of the information presented in this guide is completely new to you, then you need to supplement this guide with other sources of study materials. If you have a reasonable grounding in Oracle administration tasks, then the guide will serve to reinforce those portions that you will likely be questioned about on the exam. If you don't have any experience with Oracle at all, the compressed format of this guide is not likely to be the best method for learning. It might provide you with sufficient information to pass the test, but you're likely to have serious deficiencies as an Oracle database administrator.

Additional Study Resources

The companion website to this series is http://www.oraclecertificationprep.com. The site contains many additional resources that can be used to study for this exam (and others). From the entry page of the website, click on the 'Exams' button, and then select the link for this test. The Exam Details page contains links to the following information sources:

- Oracle documentation sources that contain significant amounts of data for this certification.
- Third-party books relevant to the exam.
- White papers and articles on Oracle Learning Library on topics covered in the exam.
- Articles on the Web that may be useful for the exam.

The website will never link to unauthorized content such as brain dumps or illegal content such as copyrighted material made available without the consent of the author. I cannot guarantee the accuracy of the content links. While I have located the data and scanned it to ensure that it is relevant to the given exam, I did not write it and have not proofread it from a technical standpoint. The material on the Oracle Learning Library is almost certain to be completely accurate and most of the other links come from highly popular Oracle support websites and are created by experienced Oracle professionals.

I recommend that you use more than one source of study materials whenever you are preparing for a certification. Reading information presented from multiple different viewpoints can help to give you a more complete picture of any given topic. The links on the website can help you to do this. Fully understanding the information covered in this certification is not just valuable so that getting a passing score is more likely – it will also help you in your career. I guarantee that in the long run, any knowledge you gain while studying for this certification will provide more benefit to you than any piece of paper or line on your resume.

Database Architecture and ASM

Oracle Database Architecture

While it is not explicitly listed among the topics for 1Z0-053, you must are liable to be asked questions that require you to understand the Oracle database architecture. This section is a review of the information that you (presumably) are aware of, having already passed 1Z0-052.

Database vs. Instance

An Oracle database server consists of two distinct components: a database and one or more database instances. In general usage, the term Oracle database is often used to refer to both. The definitions of the two are:

- **Database** – A database is a set of files, located on disk, that store data. These files can exist independently of a database instance.
- **Database instance** – An instance is a set of memory structures that manage database files. An Oracle instance consists of a shared memory area and a set of background processes. An instance can exist independently of database files.

In the conventional configuration, there is a single instance and a single database. However, when using Real Application Clusters, there are multiple instances pointing at a single database. The RAC configuration allows for improved scalability, performance, and fault tolerance.

Oracle Data Guard is a configuration where a primary database server is related to one or more standby databases. Standby databases may be physical standbys that are byte-for-byte copies of the primary and are kept current through the application of redo logs from the primary. Alternately they can be logical standbys which are kept synchronized by SQL statements propagated through Oracle Streams.

The illustration below shows the primary components of an Oracle instance.

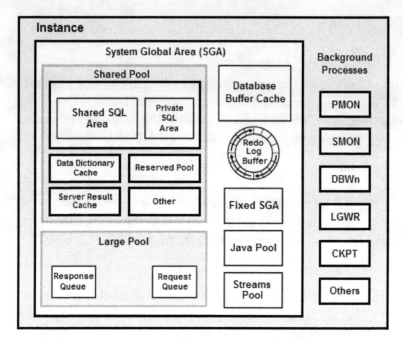

Figure 1: Oracle instance components

A database has physical and logical elements. Physical data consists of what is viewable at the operating system level. For example, database files can be listed using the **ls** command and instance processes can be listed via the Linux **ps** command. Logical data consists of data only viewable from within the database itself. You can query the data dictionary to list the tablespaces that make use of the datafiles in the operating system, but there is no Linux command that can obtain that information. The logical and physical structures of Oracle are completely separate. Renaming a tablespace does not affect the filenames of the datafiles associated with it and renaming datafiles does not affect the contents of a tablespace.

Memory Structures

When an Oracle instance is started, background processes are initiated and a memory area is allocated in the operating system. This memory area stores numerous different pieces of information required to run the database. Some of the basic memory structures are:

- **System Global Area (SGA)** – The SGA is a group of shared memory structures that contain data and control information for a single Oracle Database instance. The SGA is shared by all server and background processes. Examples of data stored in the SGA include cached data blocks and shared SQL areas.
- **Program global area (PGA)** – A PGA is a memory region that is not shared. It contains data and control information exclusively for the use of an Oracle process. A PGA is created when an Oracle process is started. One PGA exists for each server process and background process. The collection of individual PGAs is the total instance PGA, or instance PGA.
- **User Global Area (UGA)** – The UGA is memory associated with a user session.
- **Software code areas** – Software code areas are portions of memory used to store code that is being run or can be run.

System Global Area

The SGA is the memory container for all of the data required for the database instance. It consists of numerous memory components. Each component is a pool of memory used to satisfy a particular type of memory allocation request. All except the redo log buffer allocate and deallocate space in units of contiguous memory called granules. You can query the V$SGASTAT view for information about SGA components.

The most important elements of the SGA are:

- **Database Buffer Cache** – The database buffer cache stores copies of data blocks read from data files. A buffer is an address where the buffer manager temporarily caches a currently or recently used data block. All users connected to a database instance share access to the buffer cache. The buffer cache is designed to optimize physical I/O; to keep frequently accessed blocks in the buffer cache; and to write infrequently accessed blocks to disk. It makes use of a Least Recently Used (LRU) algorithm to determine what information should be kept in the buffer cache.

- **Redo Log Buffer** – The redo log buffer is a circular buffer that stores redo entries describing changes made to the database. These entries contain the information required to reconstruct changes made to the database by DML or DDL operations. Database recovery applies redo entries to data files to reconstruct lost changes. The redo entries take up continuous, sequential space in the buffer. The background process log writer (LGWR) writes the redo log buffer to the active online redo log group on disk.
- **Shared Pool** – The shared pool caches various types of program data required by the server. A partial list includes storing parsed SQL, PL/SQL code, system parameters, and data dictionary information. It is involved in almost every operation that occurs in the database. Among other things, every SQL statement issued by users requires an access of the shared pool.
- **Large Pool** – The large pool is an optional memory area in the SGA. It is intended for memory allocations that are larger than is appropriate to store in the shared pool. Examples of this are the UGA for the shared server and the Oracle XA interface and buffers for Recovery Manager (RMAN) I/O slaves.
- **Java Pool** – The Java pool stores all session-specific Java code and data within the Java Virtual Machine (JVM). This includes Java objects that are migrated to the Java session space at end-of-call.
- **Streams Pool** – The Streams pool is used exclusively by Oracle Streams. It stores buffered queue messages and provides memory for Streams capture and apply processes. Unless configured otherwise, the size of the Streams pool starts at zero and grows dynamically as required by Oracle Streams.
- **Fixed SGA** – The fixed SGA is an internal housekeeping area. Among other things, it contains general information required by the background processes about the state of the database and the instance. The size of the fixed SGA is set by the Oracle Database and cannot be altered manually.

Memory Management

Memory management is the process of maintaining optimal sizes for the Oracle instance memory structures. Ideally the size of the memory structures will change as demands on the database change. Initialization parameter settings determine how Oracle manages SGA and instance PGA memory. Oracle allocates and deallocates SGA space in units called granules, which can be 4M, 8M, or 16M in size depending on the OS.

- **Automatic Memory Management** – When using automatic memory management, Oracle manages the SGA and instance PGA memory automatically. This is the simplest method for managing memory and is strongly recommended by Oracle. For databases created with DBCA using the basic installation option, automatic memory management is enabled by default.
- **Automatic Shared Memory Management** – Automatic shared memory management enables you to exercise more control over the size of the SGA and is the default when automatic memory management is disabled. Oracle will tune the total SGA to a supplied target size and will also tune the sizes of SGA components. If you are using a server parameter file, Oracle remembers the sizes of the automatically tuned components across instance shutdowns.
- **Manual Shared Memory Management** – With Manual Shared Memory Management, you set the sizes of several individual SGA components and manually tune individual SGA components. This option provides complete control of individual SGA component sizes.

Memory Management of the Instance PGA

If automatic memory management is not enabled, then the following modes are possible for management of PGA memory:

- **Automatic PGA memory management** – If the PGA_AGGREGATE_TARGET initialization parameter is set to a nonzero value, the database uses automatic PGA memory management. In this mode, the database then tunes the size of the instance PGA to the supplied parameter value and dynamically tunes the sizes of individual PGAs. If PGA_AGGREGATE_TARGET is not explicitly set, then Oracle automatically configures a reasonable default.

- **Manual PGA memory management** – If AMM is not enabled and PGA_AGGREGATE_TARGET is explicitly set to 0, the database defaults to manual PGA management. Although Oracle Database supports the manual PGA memory management method, Oracle strongly recommends automatic PGA memory management.

Process Structures

A process is an operating system mechanism that has the ability to run a series of steps. Depending on the operating system, this may be called a job, task, or thread. Used in this context, a thread is equivalent to a process. An Oracle database instance has the following process types:

- **Client processes** – These processes run the software code for an application program or an Oracle tool.
- **Background processes** – Background processes consolidate functions that otherwise would require multiple Oracle database programs running for each client process. Background processes perform I/O and monitor other Oracle database processes.
- **Server processes** – Server processes communicate with client processes and interact with the database to fulfill requests.

Client Processes

When a user runs a program such as SQL*Developer or SQL*Plus, a client process (also known as a user process) is created by the operating system. Client processes interact with server processes in order to interface with the database. Server processes always run on the same machine as the Oracle database, while client processes generally run on a different machine. The client process has no direct access to the SGA of the database, but the servicing server process does. When the client process runs on the client machine, it is known as two-tier architecture. In some cases, the client process may run on an application server. This is known as a three-tiered architecture.

Connections vs. Sessions

Client processes must communicate with the Oracle server in order to access database information. This is done through the use of connections and sessions. The two are related, but not interchangeable.

- **Connection** – A physical communication pathway between a client process and a database instance. This pathway is created using network software or interprocess communication mechanisms. In general, a connection occurs between a client process and either a server process or a dispatcher.
- **Session** – A logical entity in the database instance that represents the state of a current user login to a database. After a user establishes a connection to a database and authenticates to a database account via a username and password, a session is established for the user. The session lasts until the user disconnects or exits the connecting application.

A single connection can generate multiple sessions. For example SQL*Developer can open multiple sessions concurrently to a given database while only requiring a single connection. A single user account can have multiple sessions open concurrently. All sessions, even those for the same user, are completely independent. The results of uncommitted transactions in one session aren't visible to another session, and issuing a commit in one session does not affect uncommitted transactions in another.

Server Processes

Server processes are created by the Oracle Database to handle the requests of client processes connected to the instance. A client process cannot communicate with the database on its own. It always communicates with the database through a separate server process. Server processes can perform the following tasks:

- Parse and run SQL statements
- Execute PL/SQL code
- Read data blocks from data files into the database buffer cache
- Return results from the database to the application

Oracle server processes can be dedicated or shared.

Dedicated Server Processes

- One client connection is associated with one server process
- The client process communicates directly with its server process
- This server process is dedicated to its client process for the duration of the session
- The server process stores process-specific information and the UGA in its PGA

Shared Server Processes

- Client applications connect to a shared dispatcher process
- The client process communicates directly with its dispatcher process
- This server processes are shared among all of the dispatcher processes
- Each shared server process has its own PGA, but not UGA.
- The UGA for a session is stored in the SGA so that any shared server can access session data

Mandatory Background Processes

The mandatory background processes are present in all typical database configurations. These processes run by default in a database instance started with a minimally configured initialization parameter file. Any processes that contain one or more n's can have multiple incarnations. Each version will be given successive integers (DBW0, DBW1, etc).

- **Process Monitor Process (PMON)** – As its name suggests, PMON monitors all of the other background processes. When a server or dispatcher process terminates abnormally, PMON performs process recovery. It is also responsible for cleaning up the database buffer cache and freeing resources that were allocated for client processes. PMON also registers information about the instance and dispatcher processes with the Oracle Net listener.
- **System Monitor Process (SMON)** – SMON is in charge of a variety of system-level cleanup duties. The duties assigned to SMON include: performing instance recovery at instance startup if

necessary; recovering any terminated transactions that were skipped during instance recovery; cleaning up unused temporary segments; and coalescing contiguous free extents within dictionary-managed tablespaces.

- **Database Writer Process (DBWn)** – DBWn processes write modified buffers in the database buffer cache to disk. All databases have at least one database writer process (DBW0). It's possible to configure additional DBWn processes to improve performance in databases with high levels of data modification. DBWn writes out to datafiles at the following times:

  - ✓ There are no free buffers.
  - ✓ Every 3 seconds
  - ✓ During a checkpoint
  - ✓ When there are too many dirty buffers
  - ✓ When the instance shuts down cleanly
  - ✓ When a tablespace changes status (i.e. is made re-only, or taken offline)

- **Log Writer Process (LGWR)** – LGWR manages the redo log buffer. LGWR writes one contiguous portion of the buffer to the online redo log. The redo log buffer is circular, once LGWR writes entries from the buffer to an online redo log file, server processes can copy new entries over the entries that were just written to disk. LGWR will write all redo entries that have been copied into the buffer since the last time it wrote if any of the following are true:

  - ✓ A user commits a transaction
  - ✓ An online redo log switch occurs
  - ✓ Three seconds have passed since LGWR last wrote
  - ✓ The redo log buffer is one-third full or contains 1 MB of buffered data
  - ✓ DBWn must write modified buffers to disk.

- **Checkpoint Process (CKPT)** – CKPT updates the control file and data file headers with checkpoint information and signals DBWn to write blocks to disk. Checkpoint information includes the checkpoint position, SCN, location in online redo log to begin recovery, and other data useful to recovery operations. CKPT performs full checkpoints only at database shutdown or on request.

- **Manageability Monitor Processes (MMON and MMNL)** – MMON performs many tasks related to the Automatic Workload Repository (AWR). For example, MMON reports when a metric violates its threshold value, takes snapshots, and captures statistics values for recently modified SQL objects. The manageability monitor lite process (MMNL) writes statistics from the Active Session History (ASH) buffer in the SGA to disk.
- **Recoverer Process (RECO)** – In a distributed database, RECO resolves failures in distributed transactions. The RECO process of a node automatically connects to other databases involved in an in-doubt distributed transaction. When a connection is reestablished, RECO automatically resolves all in-doubt transactions.

Optional Background Processes

An optional background process is any background process not defined as mandatory. The majority of optional background processes are specific to tasks or features.

- **Archiver Processes (ARCn)** – ARCn copies online redo log files to offline storage after a redo log switch occurs. The ARCn processes can also collect transaction redo data and transmit it to standby databases. ARCn processes exist only when the database is in ARCHIVELOG mode and automatic archiving is enabled.
- **Job Queue Processes (CJQ0 and Jnnn)** – Job queue processes are used to run user jobs, often in batch mode. A job is a user-defined task scheduled to run one or more times. The job coordinator process (CJQ0) is automatically started and stopped as needed by Oracle. The coordinator process dynamically spawns job queue slave processes (Jnnn) to run the jobs.
- **Flashback Data Archiver Process (FBDA)** – FBDA archives historical rows of tracked tables into Flashback Data Archives. Any time a DML transaction on a tracked table commits, FBDA stores the pre-image of the rows into the Flashback Data Archive. It also keeps metadata on the current rows.
- **Space Management Coordinator Process (SMCO)** – SMCO coordinates the execution of space management tasks, such as

proactive space allocation and space reclamation. SMCO dynamically spawns slave processes (Wnnn) to implement tasks.

Physical Storage Structures

The primary purpose of the Oracle RDBMS is to store data. This task is accomplished through the use of physical and logical storage structures. The physical database structures are the operating system files used to store the data. At the time a database is created, the following files are created:

- **Data files** – Physical data files contain all the data of the database. All logical database structures, such as tables and indexes, are physically stored in data files.
- **Control files** – Control files contains information specifying the physical structure of the database, including the database name and the names and locations of the database files. It also tracks database-wide synchronization through the use of System Change Numbers (SCNs). A common SCN between the control files and all database headers indicates the database is consistent. Control files are multiplexed, in that Oracle maintains multiple identical copies for redundancy.
- **Online redo log files** – A set of two or more online redo log files makes up an online redo log. An online redo log contains redo entries which record all changes made to data in the database. The redo log entries can be used to redo changes made to the database in the event of an instance failure. There are always two or more redo log groups in a database. When one group has been filled, LGWR points to the next log group. This is called a log switch and it does not cause a checkpoint to occur. Like control files, redo log files are multiplexed for redundancy.

There are several other files that are important for an Oracle database server, including parameter and diagnostic files. Files that are important for database recovery include backup files and archived redo log files.

Logical Storage Structures

Logical storage structures enable Oracle Database to have fine-grained control over disk space usage. The following lists the logical structures Oracle uses, from smallest to largest.

- **Data blocks** – At the finest level of granularity, data is stored in data blocks. One data block corresponds to a specific number of bytes on disk.
- **Extents** – An extent is a specific number of logically contiguous data blocks, obtained in a single allocation, and used to store a specific type of information.
- **Segments** – A segment is a set of extents allocated for a user object (for example, a table or index), undo data, or temporary data.
- **Tablespaces** – A database is divided into logical storage units called tablespaces. A tablespace is the logical container for a segment. Each tablespace contains at least one data file. Tablespaces can either be permanent or temporary. Permanent tablespaces hold permanent information such as tables and indexes. Temporary tablespaces are used for transient operations, such as sorting.

Describe Automatic Storage Management (ASM)

Oracle Automatic Storage Management (ASM) is a storage solution for Oracle Database files. It acts as a volume manager to provide a file system for the exclusive use of the database. When using ASM, partitioned disks are assigned to ASM with specifications for striping and mirroring. When making use of Automatic Storage Management, in addition to any database instances that exist, there will be an instance dedicated to ASM. Oracle ASM also makes use of the Oracle Managed Files (OMF) feature. OMF automatically creates files the locations designated, as well as naming them. It also removes the files automatically when tablespaces or files are deleted from within Oracle. The ASM instance exists to manage the disk space and distribute the I/O load across multiple drives to optimize performance. ASM provides several benefits over using standard data files:

- Simplifies operations such as creating databases and managing disk space
- Distributes data across physical disks to provide uniform performance
- Rebalances data automatically after storage configuration changes

An Oracle ASM instance uses the same basic technology as an Oracle Database instance. The System Global Area (SGA) and background processes of an ASM instance are similar to those of Oracle Database. The SGA for an ASM instance is much smaller than a database instance and has fewer internal components because the ASM instance has fewer functions. The only function of an ASM instance is to mount disk groups and make the associated file available to database instances. There is no database instance mounted by Oracle ASM instances. The logical storage elements of an Oracle ASM instance are:

- **ASM Disks** -- A storage device that is provisioned to an Oracle ASM disk group. It can be a physical disk or partition, a Logical Unit Number (LUN) from a storage array, a logical volume, or a network-attached file.
- **ASM Disk Groups** -- A collection of Oracle ASM disks managed as a logical unit.
- **ASM Files** -- A file stored in an Oracle ASM disk group. The database can store data files, control files, online redo log files, and other types of files as Oracle ASM files.
- **ASM Extents** -- The raw storage used to hold the contents of an Oracle ASM file. An ASM file consists of one or more file extents and an ASM extent consists of one or more ASM allocation units.
- **ASM Allocation Units** -- The fundamental unit of allocation within a disk group.
- **ASM Instances** -- A special Oracle instance that manages Oracle ASM disks. They manage the metadata of the disk group and provide file layout information to the database instances.

Oracle ASM supports the majority of file types required by the database. The list below shows the most commonly used file types and default template that provides the attributes for file creation. Oracle ASM cannot directly support some administrative file types on disk groups. These include trace files, audit files, alert logs, export files, and core files.

- **Control files** -- CONTROLFILE
- **Data files** -- DATAFILE
- **Redo log files** -- ONLINELOG
- **Archive log files** -- ARCHIVELOG
- **Temporary files** -- TEMPFILE
- **Data file backup pieces** -- BACKUPSET
- **Archive log backup piece** -- BACKUPSET
- **Persistent initialization parameter file (SPFILE)** -- PARAMETERFILE
- **Flashback logs** -- FLASHBACK
- **Data Pump dumpset** -- DUMPSET

Fully Qualified File Name Form

Whenever a file is created in ASM, Oracle Managed Files automatically generates a fully qualified file name for it. The fully qualified filename represents a complete path name in the Oracle ASM file system. You can use a fully qualified file name for referencing existing Oracle ASM files in Oracle ASM operations, except for disk group creation. A fully qualified file name has the following form:

+diskgroup/dbname/filetype/filetypetag.file.incarnation.

The definitions of the individual elements are:

- **+diskgroup** -- The disk group name preceded by a plus sign. The plus sign (+) is equivalent to the root directory for the Oracle ASM file system.
- **dbname** -- The DB_UNIQUE_NAME of the database to which the file belongs.
- **filetype** -- The Oracle file type and can be one of the file types shown in Table 7–3.
- **filetypetag** -- Type-specific information about the file.

- **file.incarnation** -- The file/incarnation pair, used to ensure uniqueness.

An example of a fully qualified Oracle ASM filename is:

+data/ocpdb/controlfile/Current.221.46544321

The file creation request does not specify the fully qualified filename. It supplies an alias or just a disk group name. Oracle ASM then creates the file in the correct Oracle ASM path based on the file type. ASM then assigns an appropriate fully qualified filename. If an alias is specified in the creation request, ASM creates the alias and points it to the fully qualified filename. ASM file creation requests are either single or multiple file creation requests.

Alias Filenames

Alias filenames can be used for referencing existing files and creating new ASM files. Alias names consist of the disk group name preceded by a plus sign followed by a name string. Alias filenames use a hierarchical directory structure, with the slash (/) or backslash (\) character separating name components. Aliases must include the disk group name. They cannot exist at the root level (+). When a file is created with an alias, both the alias and fully-qualified names are recorded and you can access the file with either name. Alias filenames do not (and cannot) end in a dotted pair of numbers. Examples of alias filenames include:

- +data/ocpdb/control_file_main
- +data/ocpdb/control_file_bkup
- +fra/recover/second.dbf

The example below creates an undo tablespace with a data file that has an alias name, and with attributes that are set by the user-defined template my_undo_template. This example assumes that the **ocpdb** directory has been created in disk group **data**.

```
CREATE UNDO TABLESPACE ocpundo
DATAFILE '+data/ocpdb/ocp_undo_ts' SIZE 200M;
```

If an alias is used to create the data file, it is not an Oracle Managed Files (OMF) file. This means that the file will not be automatically deleted when the tablespace is dropped. To drop the file manually after the tablespace has been dropped, use the following SQL statement:

```
ALTER DISKGROUP data DROP FILE '+data/ocpdb/ocp_undo_ts';
```

Variable ASM Allocation Units

ASM files are stored in a disk group as a group of extents. Prior to Oracle 11g a single extent mapped to a single allocation unit (AU) of a set size -- 1MB. The larger an ASM file gets, the more extents it has, and the more extent pointers are required in the SGA to describe the file. Oracle 11G reduces the number of extents required by ASM files in two ways. First, when you create a disk group in 11G, you can set the ASM Allocation Unit size to be between 1 MB and 64 MB in powers of two, such as, 1, 2, 4, 8, 16, 32, or 64. Larger AU sizes typically provide performance advantages for data warehouse applications that use large sequential reads. Second, in Oracle 11g the concept of variable size extents means that an extent can consist of one or more allocation units. The first 20,000 extents for a disk group will match the allocation unit size (1*AU). The next 20,000 extents will be made up of 8 allocation units (8*AU). Beyond that point, the extent size becomes 64 allocation units (64*AU). The combination of the two new features significantly reduces memory requirements for very large databases. The AU_SIZE attribute can be set only during disk group creation; it cannot be modified with an ALTER DISKGROUP statement.

```
CREATE DISKGROUP dgroup1A
EXTERNAL REDUNDANCY
DISK '/dev/raw/raw1a'
ATTRIBUTE 'au_size' = '16M';
```

ASM Compatibility

The COMPATIBLE.ASM attribute controls the format of data structures for ASM metadata in the given disk group. The ASM software version must be equal or greater than this value in order to be able to access the disk group. The COMPATIBLE.ASM attribute must always be greater than or equal to COMPATIBLE.RDBMS for the same disk group. For example, you can set COMPATIBLE.ASM for the disk group to 11.0 and

COMPATIBLE.RDBMS for the disk group to 10.1. In this case, the disk group can be managed only by ASM software with a version of 11.0 or higher. However, any database client of version 10.1 or higher can use the disk group. If you will be increasing both parameters, the COMPATIBLE.ASM value must be increased first.

```
ALTER DISKGROUP dgroup1A
SET ATTRIBUTE  'compatible.asm' = '11.2';
```

RDBMS Compatibility

The second of the compatibility attributes is COMPATIBLE.RDBMS. It dictates the format of messages that are exchanged between the Automatic Storage Management instance and the database instance. This parameter set the minimum database client release that may access a given disk group. You can set different values of this parameter on diskgroups within the same ASM instance for multiple database clients running at different compatibility settings. Note that the client database level is determined by the value of its own COMPATIBLE initialization parameter. A 10.1 database with a COMPATIBLE parameter value of 9.0.4 is effectively a 9.0.4 database from the standpoint of the ASM instance.

```
ALTER DISKGROUP dgroup1A
SET ATTRIBUTE  'compatible.rdbms' = '11.2';
```

When the database and ASM instances are using different software versions, the database instance supports ASM functionality of the earliest release in use. For example: A 10.1 database instance operating with an 11.1 ASM instance supports only ASM 10.1 features. Likewise, an 11.1 database instance operating with a 10.1 ASM instance supports only ASM 10.1 features.

Once either of the ASM compatible parameters for a diskgroup has been increased, it may not be set back to a lower level. You can find the compatibility levels of diskgroups in the V$ASM_DISKGROUP view:

```
SELECT group_number AS GN, name, compatibility,
       database_compatibility AS DATABASE_COMP
FROM   v$asm_diskgroup;

GN NAME          COMPATIBILITY   DATABASE_COMP
-- ----------    -------------   -------------
 1 DGROUP1A      11.1.0.0.0      11.1.0.0.0
```

Set up initialization parameter files for ASM and database instances

Set up Oracle ASM Initialization Parameters

When installing Oracle ASM in a standalone configuration, Oracle Universal Installer creates a server parameter file for the Oracle ASM instance. The ASM SPFILE is stored in a disk group during installation. For a clustered Oracle ASM environment, OUI creates a single, shared SPFILE for Oracle ASM in a disk group. It's possible to use an SPFILE or a text-based initialization parameter file (PFILE) as the Oracle ASM instance parameter file. Oracle recommends that the Oracle ASM SPFILE is placed in a disk group.

You can set ASM parameters using the Oracle ASM Configuration Assistant (ASMCA). Some parameters can be set after database creation using Oracle Enterprise Manager or SQL ALTER SYSTEM or ALTER SESSION statements. The Oracle ASM* parameters use suitable defaults for most environments. Any parameters that have names prefixed with Oracle ASM* cannot be used in database instance parameter files. There are several database initialization parameters that are also valid for an Oracle ASM instance and the default values for these are appropriate in most cases. Some of parameters for ASM instances are:

- **ASM_DISKGROUPS** -- Specifies a list of disk groups that an Oracle ASM instance mounts at startup. The default value of the ASM_DISKGROUPS parameter is a NULL string.

- **ASM_DISKSTRING** -- Specifies a comma-delimited list of strings that limits the set of disks that an Oracle ASM instance discovers. The discovery strings can include wildcard characters.
- **ASM_POWER_LIMIT** -- Specifies the default power for disk rebalancing in a disk group. The range of values is 0 to 1024. The default value is 1. A value of 0 disables rebalancing.
- **ASM_PREFERRED_READ_FAILURE_GROUPS** -- Specifies the failure groups that should be preferentially read by the given instance. Generally used for clustered Oracle ASM instances and its value can be different on different nodes.
- **DB_CACHE_SIZE** -- Determines the size of the buffer cache. Not required when using automatic memory management.
- **DIAGNOSTIC_DEST** -- Specifies the directory where diagnostics for an instance are located. The default value is the $ORACLE_BASE directory.
- **INSTANCE_TYPE** -- Set to ASM for an ASM instance.
- **LARGE_POOL_SIZE** -- Specifies the size of the LARGE_POOL memory area. Not required when using automatic memory management.
- **PROCESSES** -- This parameter affects Oracle ASM, but the default value is usually suitable.

SHARED_POOL_SIZE -- Determines the amount of memory required to manage the instance. The setting for this parameter is also used to determine the amount of space that is allocated for extent storage. Not required when using automatic memory management.

Set up Oracle Database Initialization Parameters

When an Oracle instance starts, it makes use of an initialization parameter file to determine many of the database settings that will be used. At minimum, this file must specify the DB_NAME parameter. If the file contains nothing else, all other parameters will be set to default values. There are two types of parameter file that Oracle can use: a text-based parameter file that is read-only to the Oracle instance (PFILE), or a binary file that the instance can both read from and write to (SPFILE). Oracle uses the following steps to locate an initialization parameter file during startup. It will use the first file it locates:

1. It looks for spfile[SID].ora
2. It looks for spfile.ora
3. It looks for init[SID].ora

The recommended option is to utilize the binary file. It is called a server parameter file or spfile. Unlike the text-based pfile, with a spfile, you can change initialization parameters using ALTER SYSTEM commands and have those changes persist across a database shutdown and startup. The spfile also provides a method by which Oracle can self-tune. A spfile can be created manually from your text-based initialization file. Alternately, DBCA can automatically generate one when the database is created.

Common Initialization Parameters

The following are all commonly set initialization parameters. These and other initialization parameters are listed in more detail in the Oracle 11G Reference Manual.

- **DB_NAME** – Determines the local component of the database name.
- **DB_DOMAIN** – Indicates the domain (logical location) within a network structure. This parameter is optional. The combination of the DB_NAME and DB_DOMAIN must create a database name that is unique within a network
- **CONTROL_FILES** – Specifies one or more control filenames for the database. Control files are generated at the time a database is created using the names specified by the CONTROL_FILES parameter. If you do not include CONTROL_FILES in the initialization parameter file, Oracle will create a control file in the same directory as the initialization parameter file using a default operating system–dependent filename.
- **PROCESSES** – Determines the maximum number of OS processes that can connect to Oracle simultaneously. At minimum, this parameter must have a minimum value of one for each background process plus one for each user process.

- **MEMORY_TARGET** – Sets a target memory size for the instance. The total memory used by the instance will remain reasonably constant, based on the supplied value. The instance will automatically distribute memory between the system global area (SGA) and the instance program global area (instance PGA).
- **SGA_TARGET** – If MEMORY_TARGET is not set, you can enable the automatic shared memory management feature by setting the SGA_TARGET parameter to a nonzero value. This parameter sets the total size of the SGA. Oracle will automatically tune the SGA components as needed.
- **SGA_MAX_SIZE** – Specifies the maximum size of the System Global Area for the lifetime of the instance. If you do not specify SGA_MAX_SIZE, then Oracle Database selects a default value that is the sum of all components specified or defaulted at the time of initialization.
- **PGA_AGGREGATE_TARGET** – Allows you to control the total amount of memory dedicated to the instance PGA.
- **UNDO_MANAGEMENT** – When set to AUTO or null, this parameter enables automatic undo management. When set to MANUAL, undo management will use manual mode.
- **UNDO_TABLESPACE** – This parameter is optional, and valid only in automatic undo management mode. The parameter specifies the name of an undo tablespace. It is used only when the database has multiple undo tablespaces.
- **DB_BLOCK_SIZE** – Sets the standard block size for the database. The standard block size is used for the SYSTEM tablespace and will be used for other tablespaces by default. Oracle can support up to four additional nonstandard block sizes.
- **COMPATIBLE** – Used to make Oracle act as if it were an earlier release of the software.
- **DIAGNOSTIC_DEST** – Used to determine the location of the Automatic Diagnostic Repository.
- **LOG_ARCHIVE_DEST_n** – Determines where to write Archived Redo Logs.
- **OPEN_CURSORS** – Sets the maximum number of open cursors for an individual session.
- **SESSIONS** – Sets the maximum number of sessions that can connect to the database.

Start up and shut down ASM instances

Starting an Oracle ASM Instance

An Oracle ASM instance is started much like an Oracle database instance with some minor differences. When starting an Oracle ASM instance, note the following:

You must set the ORACLE_SID environment variable to the Oracle ASM system identifier (SID). The default Oracle ASM SID for a single-instance database is +ASM, and the default SID for Oracle ASM for an Oracle RAC node is +ASMnode_number where node_number is the number of the node. The ORACLE_HOME environment variable must be set to the Grid Infrastructure home where Oracle ASM was installed.

- The initialization parameter file must contain the following entry: INSTANCE_TYPE = ASM. This indicates that it is an Oracle ASM instance rather than a database instance.
- When you run the STARTUP command, rather than trying to mount and open a database, this command attempts to mount Oracle ASM disk groups.

An ASM instance interprets SQL*Plus STARTUP command parameters differently than a database instance.

- **FORCE** -- Issues a SHUTDOWN ABORT to the Oracle ASM instance before restarting it.
- **MOUNT or OPEN** -- Mounts the disk groups specified in the ASM_DISKGROUPS initialization parameter. This is the default. An OPEN state for an ASM instance doesn't really exist. If supplied, this parameter is simply treated as MOUNT.
- **NOMOUNT** -- Starts up the Oracle ASM instance without mounting any disk groups.
- **RESTRICT** -- Starts up an instance in restricted mode. Only users with both the CREATE SESSION and RESTRICTED SESSION system privileges can connect.

The SYSASM operating system privilege and the OSASM operating system group allow storage responsibilities to be assigned to System

Administrators without granting high-level access to the Oracle database itself. Users can be created in the ASM instance and granted the SYSASM privilege. This allows them to connect to the ASM instance and perform administration tasks. Similarly, assigning an operating system user to the OSASM group would allow then to connect as SYSASM using OS authentication.

```
$ export ORACLE_SID=+ASM
$ sqlplus / as sysasm

CREATE USER asm_admin IDENTIFIED by badpassword_nobiscuit;
User created.

SQL> GRANT SYSASM TO asm_admin;


SQLPLUS /NOLOG
SQL> CONNECT asm_admin AS SYSASM
Enter password: badpassword_nobiscuit
Connected to an idle instance.

SQL> STARTUP
ASM instance started
Total System Global Area 71303168 bytes
Fixed Size 1069292 bytes
Variable Size 45068052 bytes
ASM Cache 25165824 bytes
ASM disk groups mounted
```

Shutting Down an Oracle ASM Instance

An ASM instance is shut down using the SHUTDOWN command in SQL*Plus just as with a database instance. As with startup, you must ensure that the ORACLE_SID environment variable is set to the Oracle ASM SID before connecting to SQL*Plus. Before you shut down an ASM instance, you should shut down all database instances that use it. You should also dismount all file systems mounted on Oracle ASM Dynamic Volume Manager volumes before attempting to shut down the ASM instance.

To shut down an Oracle ASM instance, perform the following steps:

```
SQLPLUS /NOLOG
SQL> CONNECT asm_admin AS SYSASM
Enter password: badpassword_nobiscuit
Connected.
```

```
SQL> SHUTDOWN NORMAL
```

The SHUTDOWN modes when used with an Oracle ASM instance are:

- **NORMAL** -- The instance waits for any in-progress SQL to complete before dismounting all of the disk groups and shutting down. The instance also waits for all currently connected users to disconnect from the instance. If any database instances are connected to the ASM instance, then the SHUTDOWN command aborts and returns an error. NORMAL is the default mode.
- **IMMEDIATE or TRANSACTIONAL** -- The instance waits for any in-progress SQL to complete before dismounting all of the disk groups and shutting down the Oracle ASM instance. It does not wait for users currently connected to the instance to disconnect. If any database instances are connected to the Oracle ASM instance, then the SHUTDOWN aborts with an error. ASM instances have no transactions, so TRANSACTIONAL and IMMEDIATE are equivalent.
- **ABORT** -- The instance immediately shuts down without the orderly dismount of disk groups. This requires recovery on the next Oracle ASM startup. Any database instances that are connected to the Oracle ASM instance will also perform a shutdown abort because their storage will no longer be available.

Administer ASM disk groups

An ASM disk group consists of multiple disks and is the fundamental object that Oracle ASM manages. Disk groups contain the information required to manage drive space. The sub-components of disk groups include disks, files, and allocation units. A given file is contained within a single disk group. However, a disk group can contain files from several databases. A single database can use files from multiple disk groups.

Disk Group Attributes

Disk group attributes are parameters that are bound to a disk group rather than an Oracle ASM instance. Some of the more common attributes are below. Refer to the Oracle ASM Administrator's Guide for more details.

- **ACCESS_CONTROL.ENABLED** -- This attribute determines whether Oracle ASM File Access Control is enabled for a disk group. The value can be true or false. The default is false. This attribute can only be set when altering a disk group.
- **ACCESS_CONTROL.UMASK** -- This attribute determines which permissions are masked out on the creation of an Oracle ASM file for the user that owns the file, users in the same user group, and others not in the user group. This attribute applies to all files on a disk group.
- **AU_SIZE** -- A file extent consists of one or more allocation units. An Oracle ASM file consists of one or more file extents. When you create a disk group, you can set the Oracle ASM allocation unit size with the AU_SIZE disk group attribute. The values can be 1, 2, 4, 8, 16, 32, or 64 MB, depending on the specific disk group compatibility level.
- **COMPATIBLE.ASM** -- This attribute controls the format of data structures for ASM metadata in the given disk group. The ASM software version must be equal or greater than this value in order to be able to access the disk group. The COMPATIBLE.ASM attribute must always be greater than or equal to COMPATIBLE.RDBMS for the same disk group. For example, you can set COMPATIBLE.ASM for the disk group to 11.0 and COMPATIBLE.RDBMS for the disk group to 10.1. In this case, the disk group can be managed only by ASM software with a version of 11.0 or higher. However, any database client of version 10.1 or higher can use the disk group. If you will be increasing both parameters, the COMPATIBLE.ASM value must be increased first.
- **COMPATIBLE.RDBMS** -- This dictates the format of messages that are exchanged between the Automatic Storage Management instance and the database instance. This parameter set the minimum database client release that may access a given disk group. You can set different values of this parameter on diskgroups within the same ASM instance for multiple database clients running at different compatibility settings.
- **CONTENT.TYPE** -- Identifies the disk group type: data, recovery, or system. The type value determines the distance to the nearest neighbor disk in the failure group where Oracle ASM mirrors

copies of the data. The default value is 'data' which specifies a distance of 1 to the nearest neighbor disk. A value of 'recovery' specifies a distance of 3 to the nearest neighbor disk and a value of 'system' specifies a distance of 5.

- **DISK_REPAIR_TIME** -- Determines the amount of time that a disk can be unavailable due to a transient failure before to being dropped permanently from the diskgroup. To use this parameter, both the compatible.rdbms and compatible.asm attributes must be set to at least 11.1. You cannot set this attribute when creating a disk group, but you can alter the DISK_REPAIR_TIME attribute in an ALTER DISKGROUP ... SET ATTRIBUTE statement to change the default value. If both compatible.rdbms and compatible.asm are set to at least 11.1, then the default is 3.6 hours. If either parameter is less than 11.1, the disk is dropped immediately if it becomes inaccessible. The time can be specified in units of minutes by using the letter M or hours by using the letter H. If you provide a number with no unit, then the default is hours. The default attribute value can be changed while bringing the disk offline by using an ALTER DISKGROUP ... DISK OFFLINE statement and the DROP AFTER clause. If a disk is taken offline using the current value of DISK_REPAIR_TIME, and the value of this attribute for the diskgroup is subsequently changed with the ALTER DISKGROUP ... SET ATTRIBUTE statement, then the changed value is used by ASM in determining when to drop the disk.

CREATE DISKGROUP

The CREATE DISKGROUP SQL statement is used to create disk groups. When creating a disk group, you specify the following information:

- A unique name to the disk group.
- The redundancy level of the disk group. For Oracle ASM to mirror files, specify the redundancy level as NORMAL REDUNDANCY (2-way mirroring by default for most file types) or HIGH REDUNDANCY (3-way mirroring for all files). Specify EXTERNAL REDUNDANCY if you do not want mirroring by Oracle ASM.
- The disks that are to be formatted as Oracle ASM disks belonging to the disk group.
- Optionally specify the disks as belonging to specific failure groups.

- Optionally specify the type of failure group.
- Optionally specify disk group attributes, such as software compatibility or allocation unit size.

The SQL statement below creates a disk group named data with normal redundancy. It consists of two failure groups: fg1 or fg2 with three disks in each failure group. The data disk group is typically used to store database data files.

```
CREATE DISKGROUP data NORMAL REDUNDANCY
FAILGROUP fg1 DISK
'/devices/diska1' NAME diska1,
'/devices/diska2' NAME diska2,
'/devices/diska3' NAME diska3
FAILGROUP fg2 DISK
'/devices/diskb1' NAME diskb1,
'/devices/diskb2' NAME diskb2,
'/devices/diskb3' NAME diskb3
ATTRIBUTE 'au_size'='2M',
'compatible.asm' = '11.2',
'compatible.rdbms' = '11.2';
```

ALTER DISKGROUP

The ALTER DISKGROUP SQL statement enables you to alter a disk group configuration. It is possible to add, resize, or drop disks while the database remains online. Multiple operations in a single ALTER DISKGROUP statement are both possible and recommended. Grouping operations in a single ALTER DISKGROUP statement can reduce rebalancing operations. Oracle ASM automatically rebalances a disk group when its configuration changes. The V$ASM_OPERATION view allows you to monitor the status of rebalance operations. The following command adds two more disks to the data diskgroup.

```
ALTER DISKGROUP data ADD DISK
'/devices/diska4' NAME diska4,
'/devices/diska5' NAME diska5;
```

Configuring for Recoverability

One of the primary tasks for an Oracle DBA is to ensure that the information stored in the database is not lost. The capabilities built into the database engine combined with a robust backup strategy should ensure that committed transactions will be recoverable under almost any failure scenario. For any database that has data worth of recovering (i.e. pretty much anything except a testing platform), the database should be in ARCHIVELOG mode.

The initial archiving mode of Oracle is set in the CREATE DATABASE statement. The default is for the database to be in NOARCHIVELOG mode. Archiving the redo information generated by database creation is of no value, so the default is almost always used. After database creation, the mode should generally be changed to ARCHIVELOG.

The archiving mode of the database is set via the ALTER DATABASE statement with the ARCHIVELOG or NOARCHIVELOG clause. You must be connected to the database with SYSDBA privileges and the database must be mounted, but not open.

The steps to switch the database from NOARCHIVELOG to ARCHIVELOG are:

- **Shut down the database** -- The database must first be closed and any associated instances shut down.
- **Back up the database** -- The database should always be backed up before making major changes.
- **Set Parameters** -- You must edit the initialization parameter file to specify the archived redo log file destinations.
- **Start the instance in mount mode** -- The database cannot be open when changing the archive status.
- **Change the mode** -- Issue the ALTER DATABASE ARCHIVELOG command to place the database in archiving mode
- **Open the database** -- Issue an ALTER DATABASE OPEN.
- **Shut down the database** -- Issue a SHUTDOWN IMMEDIATE to shut down the instance and close the database.

- **Back up the database** -- You must back up all database files and the control file. Any previous backups cannot be used with the archived redo logs for recovery because they were not taken in ARCHIVELOG mode.

Configure multiple archive log file destinations to increase availability

When the database is in archivelog mode, at least one destination for archived log files must be specified. However, it is possible to specify two or more destinations to provide greater redundancy. The destinations can be either to a local file system, a remote file system, or to an Oracle Automatic Storage Management (Oracle ASM) disk group. If multiple destinations are specified, a copy of each filled redo log file will be written out to every destination simultaneously. If there is a failure at one of the destinations, Oracle can make use of a copy from one of the alternate destinations during recovery.

There are two methods by which you can set the archive log file destination.

- **LOG_ARCHIVE_DEST and LOG_ARCHIVE_DUPLEX_DEST** -- For a single archive log destination, you can set only the LOG_ARCHIVE_DEST initialization parameters. To maintain a primary and secondary destination, you would specify the duplex location. These parameters can only be used for locations on the local host. Some examples are:

```
LOG_ARCHIVE_DEST = '/u01/arc'
LOG_ARCHIVE_DUPLEX_DEST = '/u02/arc'
```

- **LOG_ARCHIVE_DEST_n** -- If you wish to archive to three or more locations, you must use the alternate LOG_ARCHIVE_DEST_n initialization parameters. The value of n can be any integer from 1 to 31. Archive destinations 1 to 10 are available for local or remote locations. Archive destinations 11 to 31 are available for remote locations only. Some examples are:

```
LOG_ARCHIVE_DEST_1 = 'LOCATION=/u01/arc'
LOG_ARCHIVE_DEST_2 = 'LOCATION=/u02/arc'
LOG_ARCHIVE_DEST_3 = 'LOCATION=/u03/arc'
```

The LOCATION keyword for LOG_ARCHIVE_DEST_n can be used to specify a file system location on the current host, an Oracle ASM disk group, or the Fast Recovery Area. Examples of each of these are:

```
LOG_ARCHIVE_DEST_n = 'LOCATION=/u01/arc'
LOG_ARCHIVE_DEST_n = 'LOCATION=+DGROUP1'
LOG_ARCHIVE_DEST_n = 'LOCATION=USE_DB_RECOVERY_FILE_DEST'
```

Alternately, the SERVICE keyword for LOG_ARCHIVE_DEST_n can be used to specify remote archival through an Oracle Net service name. An example of which is:

```
LOG_ARCHIVE_DEST_n = 'SERVICE=remotedb'
```

Adding the MANDATORY keyword to a log archive destination specifies that archiving to the given destination must succeed before the redo log file can be made available for reuse

```
LOG_ARCHIVE_DEST_1 = 'LOCATION=/u01/arc MANDATORY'
```

Define, apply and use a retention policy

RMAN retention policies are intended to insure that you have sufficient redundancy in the number of database backups to prevent a catastrophic data loss while keeping you from storing so many that you run out of disk space. The RMAN command CONFIGURE RETENTION POLICY is used to define an automatic backup retention policy. The backup retention policy provides RMAN with the information required to decide if a given backup of datafiles or control files is obsolete. Obsolete backups are no longer needed for recovery. These files can be viewed using the REPORT OBSOLETE command or removed using the DELETE OBSOLETE command.

Even when a retention policy is in place, RMAN will never automatically delete backup files simply because they have become obsolete. The files will remain until removed via the DELETE OBSOLETE command. However, if a database has been configured with a fast recovery area, it is possible that obsolete files can be deleted to satisfy the flash recovery area disk quota rules. If additional space is needed for new files then the database will delete files in the fast recovery area that are either obsolete or have already been backed up to tape. However, the database will <u>not</u> violate the retention policy in order to free up space in the fast recovery area.

Obsolete recovery files should not be confused with expired files. The two have different definitions:

- **Obsolete** -- Backup files are obsolete when according to the current retention policy, they are no longer required for recovery.

- **Expired** -- Backup files are set to expired when an RMAN CROSSCHECK operation is performed and the file cannot be located.

Only control file backups and full or level 0 datafile backups are directly subject to retention policies. If datafiles are part of a backup set, RMAN cannot delete the set until <u>all</u> of the datafile backups within it are obsolete. For individual datafile copies or proxy copies, RMAN can delete them as soon as it is no longer needed according to the policy.

Incremental level 1 backups and archived redo logs become obsolete when no full backups exist that require them. RMAN initially determines which datafile and control file backups are obsolete. All incremental level 1 backups and archived logs that are not required to recover the remaining (non-obsolete) datafile or control file backup are tagged as obsolete. When using a retention policy, backup files should not be removed via non-RMAN utilities. If disk or tape files are removed via OS or media manager commands then this invalidates the ability of RMAN to intelligently control the retention of files.

There are two different types of retention policy. It is only possible to use <u>one</u> of them -- they are mutually exclusive.

- **Recovery Window** -- This is a rolling window of time starting with the present and extending backward in time for a set length. A recovery window defines a point of recoverability, which will be the earliest time from which it is possible to recover following a media failure. If the defined recovery window is two weeks, then RMAN retains full backups and required incremental backups and archived logs that will allow the database to be recovered up to 14 days in the past. A recovery window policy is implemented as follows:

```
CONFIGURE RETENTION POLICY TO RECOVERY WINDOW OF 14
DAYS;
```

- **Backup Redundancy** -- The redundancy retention policy specifies the number backups of each datafile to be retained. When there are more available than the number required, the oldest backups beyond the defined number are obsolete. The default retention policy is configured to REDUNDANCY 1. A backup redundancy of 3 is implemented as follows:

```
CONFIGURE RETENTION POLICY TO REDUNDANCY 3;
```

Use Fast Recovery Area

In version 11.2, the 'Flash Recovery Area' was renamed to 'Fast Recovery Area'. Much of the documentation (and the test topics on the Oracle Education site) still use the older terminology. You might see either name in the test. They mean the same thing. The recovery area was renamed to avoid giving the impression that this area is primarily for Flashback operations.

The Fast Recovery Area is a location in which the database can store and manage files related to backup and recovery. The location is separate from the database area, where the current database files are located. The fast recovery area can contain control files, online redo logs, archived redo logs, flashback logs, and RMAN backups. Files in the recovery area are labeled as permanent or transient.

- **Permanent files** -- These are active files used by the database instance. Permanent files that can be in the recovery area include multiplexed copies of the current control file and online redo log files.

- **Transient files** -- These files are not accessed by the database instance and are needed only during recovery operations. Transient files include: archived redo log files, foreign archived redo log files, image copies of datafiles and control files, backup pieces, and flashback logs.

Transient files are generally deleted after they become obsolete or have been backed up to tape. Files placed in the fast recovery area are maintained by Oracle Database and the generated file names use the Oracle Managed Files (OMF) format. When files are no longer needed for recovery, they become eligible for deletion when space for new files is required.

Managing Space in the Fast Recovery Area

The database issues a warning alert when reclaimable space is less than 15% and a critical alert when reclaimable space is less than 3%. An entry is added to the alert log and to the DBA_OUTSTANDING_ALERTS table to warn the DBA of this condition. If not resolved, the database will consume space in the fast recovery area until there is no space left.

You can resolve low space issues in the Fast Recovery Area in several ways:

- Make more disk space available and increase DB_RECOVERY_FILE_DEST_SIZE.

- Move backups from the fast recovery area to tertiary storage such as tape. The BACKUP RECOVERY AREA command will back up all of your recovery area files to tape.
- Run DELETE for any files that have been removed with an operating system utility. The database is not aware of file removed by OS commands.
- Run the RMAN CROSSCHECK command to have RMAN recheck the contents of the fast recovery area and identify expired files, and then use the DELETE EXPIRED command to delete every expired backup from the RMAN repository.
- Delete any unnecessary guaranteed restore points.
- Review your backup retention policy and make it less restrictive.

Information about the Fast Recovery Area is stored in the V$RECOVERY_FILE_DEST dynamic view. In addition, the column IS_RECOVERY_DET_FILE has been added to the following views: V$CONTROLFILE, V$LOGFILE, V$ARCHIVED_LOG, V$DATAFILE_COPY, V$DATAFILE, V$BACKUP_PIECE and the RMAN tables. This column has a value of YES if a file of the corresponding kind has been created in the fast recovery area.

Configure the Fast Recovery Area

The following initialization parameters are used to enable the Fast Recovery Area. Only the first two are required, and the database does not require a restart after they have been set.

- **DB_RECOVERY_FILE_DEST_SIZE** -- Specifies the maximum total bytes to be used by the Fast Recovery Area. The basic (minimum) recovery area size should be the sum of all the database files, plus sufficient size for incremental backups and all archive logs that have not been copied to tape. The required size varies widely depending on the backup strategy and whether flashback retention is enabled. This initialization parameter must be specified before DB_RECOVERY_FILE_DEST is enabled.

- **DB_RECOVERY_FILE_DEST** -- Location of the Fast Recovery Area. This can be a directory, file system, or Automatic Storage Management (Oracle ASM) disk group. It cannot be a raw file system.
- **DB_FLASHBACK_RETENTION_TARGET** -- Specifies the upper limit (in minutes) on how far back in time the database may be flashed back. This parameter is required only for Flashback Database.

These parameters cannot be enabled if you have set values for the parameters LOG_ARCHIVE_DEST and LOG_ARCHIVE_DUPLEX_DEST. You must disable those parameters before setting up the Fast Recovery Area. You must instead set values for the LOG_ARCHIVE_DEST_n parameters.

Oracle recommends that archive logs be written to the fast recovery area so that the archived logs are automatically managed by the database. Because the fast recovery area is managed by OMF, the generated file names for the archived logs are not determined by the parameter LOG_ARCHIVE_FORMAT. Whether the fast recovery area is used or not, it is always best practice to create multiple copies of archived redo logs.

The following basic options for archiving redo logs are possible, listed in descending order of what Oracle considers to be best practice:

- Enable archiving to the fast recovery area only and use disk mirroring for redundancy. If DB_RECOVERY_FILE_DEST is specified and no LOG_ARCHIVE_DEST_n is specified, then LOG_ARCHIVE_DEST_1 is implicitly set to the recovery area.
- Enable archiving to the fast recovery area and set one or more LOG_ARCHIVE_DEST_n initialization parameters to locations outside the fast recovery area. The fast recovery area can be set as an archiving destination by setting any LOG_ARCHIVE_DEST_n parameter to LOCATION=USE_DB_RECOVERY_FILE_DEST.
- Set LOG_ARCHIVE_DEST_n initialization parameters to archive only to non-fast recovery area locations.

Using the RMAN Recovery Catalog

Identify situations that require RMAN recovery catalog

The RMAN recovery catalog is a database schema in an Oracle database that is used to store metadata about one or more Oracle databases. The data from this schema is used by RMAN when performing recovery operations. While the catalog can be stored in a database used for other purposes, it is generally stored in a dedicated database. The catalog stores information about RMAN operations for all of the target databases that have been registered in it. Any time that RMAN is connected to a recovery catalog, all metadata will be pulled exclusively from the catalog instead of the control file. By centralizing the metadata for all your target databases, the recovery catalog makes reporting and administration easier. A recovery catalog includes:

- Datafile and archived redo log backup sets and backup pieces
- Datafile copies
- Archived redo logs and their copies
- Database structure (tablespaces and datafiles)
- Stored scripts, which are named user-created sequences of RMAN commands
- Persistent RMAN configuration settings

Recovery files are required in the following cases:

- **Loss of control files** -- If the current control file and all backups are lost for a given database, a recovery catalog is required. Recovery catalogs contain the same metadata as the RMAN repository stored in the control file of each target database.
- **Recovery from very old backup** -- The control file contains a more limited amount of history than a recovery catalog. If you need to perform a recovery from a backup that goes back further in time

than is stored in the control file, then a recovery catalog is required.

- **RMAN Scripts** -- RMAN scripts can be stored in a recovery catalog. The scripts are then available to every RMAN client that can connect to the target database and recovery catalog. By contrast, command files are only available if the RMAN client has access to the file system on which they are stored.
- **Data Guard** -- If you want to use RMAN in a Data Guard environment, a recovery catalog is required. The recovery catalog stores RMAN metadata for all primary and standby databases.

Create and configure a recovery catalog

Before creating a recovery catalog, you must determine what database to put it in and what schema to use. You should not put the catalog in a database that will itself be a target of the catalog. Using a dedicated catalog database is the normal and suggested option. In addition, the catalog database should not be on the same hard drive as any of its target databases or a single hard drive failure can take out both the target database and the catalog required to recover the target. The greater the independence between the catalog and target databases, the more robust the recovery scenario becomes. Once a database is selected, the catalog will be stored in a schema on that database (which cannot be SYS).

The space required by the catalog schema depends primarily on the number of databases that will be targets of the catalog. The size will also increase as the number of backups and archived log files for each individual database grows. RMAN scripts stored in the catalog will use space as well. The Oracle Database Backup and Recovery User's Guide contains more information and formulas on estimating size requirements.

Once a catalog database and schema have been determined and sufficient space exists in the catalog tablespace, you can create the schema owner and grant the schema all of the privileges required. In the example below, a dedicated database (catdb) with a tablespace called RMANCAT_TS exists. The SYS user has connected to catdb with SYSDBA privileges.

To create the recovery catalog schema and set up the default and temporary tablespaces:

```
SQL>  CREATE USER recodude IDENTIFIED BY [password]
      TEMPORARY TABLESPACE temp
      DEFAULT TABLESPACE rmancat_ts
      QUOTA UNLIMITED ON rmancat_ts;
```

Grant the RECOVERY_CATALOG_OWNER role to the rman schema.

```
SQL> GRANT RECOVERY_CATALOG_OWNER TO recodude;
```

Once the catalog schema exists, the RMAN CREATE CATALOG command is used to create the catalog tables in the default tablespace of the catalog owner. To create the recovery catalog you must start RMAN and connect to the catalog database as the recovery catalog owner. Once connected, run the CREATE CATALOG command to create the catalog. This can take several minutes.

```
RMAN> CREATE CATALOG;
```

You can specify the tablespace name for the catalog in the CREATE CATALOG command to store it in a tablespace other than the default for the schema:

```
RMAN> CREATE CATALOG TABLESPACE users;
```

Registering a Database

Once a catalog exists, you must register the target databases in the catalog. Until a database has been registered, RMAN cannot store any metadata about backup operations in the catalog. Unregistered databases will continue to use the control file as their sole source of RMAN metadata during backup and recovery operations. To register a new target database, you must:

Start RMAN and connect to both the target database and to the recovery catalog. The database contained the recovery catalog must be open and the target database must be mounted.

```
% rman TARGET / CATALOG recodude@catdb
```

Register the target database in the connected recovery catalog via the REGISTER DATABASE command:

```
REGISTER DATABASE;
```

RMAN will add information about the target database to the appropriate catalog tables. It then copies information from the control file of the target database into the catalog to synchronize the catalog with the control file. Once the command has completed, you can verify that the registration was successful by running the REPORT SCHEMA command:

```
REPORT SCHEMA;

Report of database schema
File Size(MB)    Tablespace   RB segs Datafile Name
---- ---------- ----------- ------- ------------------
1        327680 SYSTEM          NO   /u01/oradata/system01.dbf
2         30720 UNDOTBS         YES  /u01/oradata/undotbs01.dbf
3         20480 INDEX_TS        NO   /u01/oradata/index_ts01.dbf
4         10240 TOOLS_TS        NO   /u01/oradata/tools_ts01.dbf
5         20480 USER_TS         NO   /u01/oradata/user_ts01.dbf
```

When you first create the recovery catalog, it is possible that you have datafile copies, backup pieces, or archived logs on disk that have aged out of the control file. It is possible to add them to the recovery catalog with the CATALOG command. Doing this allows RMAN to make use of use the older backups during restore operations. The following commands can be used to add files to the catalog:

- **CATALOG DATAFILECOPY** -- Allows you to add a data file backup to the catalog.
- **CATALOG ARCHIVELOG** -- Allows you to add one or more archived log files to the catalog.
- **CATALOG BACKUPPIECE** -- Allows you to add a backup piece to the catalog.

- **CATALOG START WITH** -- Allows you to add multiple files from a given directory to the catalog. RMAN will list the files to be added to the RMAN repository and prompts for confirmation before adding the backups.

When using the CATALOG START WITH command, you should be aware that if multiple directory paths contain the text supplied, you may catalog files that did not intend to. Consider a file system that has one directory called **/u01/backups** and another called **/u01/backups/old** that contain backup files. Issuing the following command catalogs all files in both directories:

```
CATALOG START WITH '/u01/backups';
```

To catalog only backups in the /u01/backups directory, the correct command should be:

```
CATALOG START WITH '/u01/backups/';
```

Synchronize the recovery catalog

Synchronizing the recovery catalog is the process of comparing the recovery catalog to the control file (either the current or the backup) and updating the catalog with any metadata that has been changed or is not present on the catalog. RMAN automatically resynchronizes the catalog when most commands are issued, so long as the target control file is mounted and the catalog is available. It is possible to perform a full or a partial resynchronization of the catalog.

- **Partial** -- During a partial resynchronization, RMAN will update changed metadata about new backups, new archived redo logs, and so on from the target control file. Metadata in the catalog about the database physical schema will not be updated.

- **Full** -- In a full resynchronization, RMAN will locate and update all changed metadata records, including those for the database schema. A full resynchronization is performed only after structural changes have been made to the database (such as changes to database files) or if the RMAN persistent configuration has been altered.

During a full resynchronization, RMAN will create a temporary backup called a snapshot control file. This file is used to ensure that RMAN has a consistent view of the control file. It is intended only to be used for a short period of time and is not registered in the catalog. The control file checkpoint is maintained in the recovery catalog to verify the catalog currency.

If RMAN is connected to the target database and the recovery catalog, it will automatically resynchronize the recovery catalog whenever commands are executed. You should seldom need to manually resynchronize the catalog. However, there are times when it is required:

- **Catalog Unavailability** -- If you issue RMAN commands at a time when the recovery catalog is unavailable, you should open the catalog database later and use the RESYNC CATALOG command to resynchronize it manually. This might be the case if your target database and catalog database are in different locations and the availability of both at the same time cannot be guaranteed.
- **Infrequent Backups** -- If a target database running in ARCHIVELOG mode is backed up infrequently, it possible that a significant number of redo logs are archived between database backups. The recovery catalog is not updated automatically when a redo log switch occurs or when a redo log is archived. Metadata about redo log switches and archived redo logs is stored only in the control file. When RMAN backup operations are infrequent, you should regularly issue a RESYNC CATALOG to ensure this information is stored in the recovery catalog.
- **Standby Database** -- It is possible to create or alter the RMAN configuration for a standby database while not connected to the database as TARGET. After doing so, to update the control file of

the standby database you can resynchronize the standby database manually.

- **Prevent Loss of Metadata** -- The data in the recovery catalog originates from the control file and the data in the control file is only kept for a limited time before being overwritten. You must ensure that the catalog is synchronized with the control file before uncataloged metadata gets overwritten. The initialization parameter CONTROL_FILE_RECORD_KEEP_TIME sets the minimum number of days that records are guaranteed to be kept in the control file. The catalog must be resynchronized at intervals less than that value by either performing backup operations that implicitly resynchronize the catalog or performing manual resynchronizations.

The RESYNC CATALOG command forces a full resynchronization of the recovery catalog. The steps to perform this are:

- Start RMAN and connect to a target database and recovery catalog.
- Mount or open the target database if it is not already mounted or open via the STARTUP MOUNT command.
- Resynchronize the recovery catalog using the RESYNC CATALOG command at the RMAN prompt.

Create and Use RMAN stored scripts

RMAN recovery catalogs allow for the creation of stored scripts. Stored scripts act much like RMAN command files. However, command files require access to the file system where they are saved, whereas stored scripts require only a connection to the catalog. The CREATE SCRIPT command is used to create a stored script in the recovery catalog. It allows you to create a named sequence of RMAN commands in the recovery catalog for later execution. The CREATE SCRIPT command can only be executed from the RMAN prompt while connected to a target

database and an open recovery catalog. Stored scripts can be either
Global or Local:

- **GLOBAL** -- A global script is available for use with any database
  registered in the recovery catalog. Global scripts are available to
  virtual private catalogs with read-only access. It is only possible to
  create or update global scripts while connected to the base
  recovery catalog.

- **LOCAL** -- Local scripts created for the current target database
  only. They are not available to virtual private catalogs.

Local and Global scripts have different namespaces. It is possible to have a
local and a global script of the same name. It is not possible to have two
global scripts of the same name or two local scripts of the same name for
a given target database.

Stored scripts can make use of substitution variables. &1 indicates where
to place the first value, &2 indicate where to place the second value, and
so on. If any special characters are included, they must be quoted. The
syntax for substitution variables is &integer followed by an optional
period. When the substitution variable is parsed, the optional period is
replaced with the value. This allows the substitution text to be followed
by another integer. In the following three cases, the value **orcl_backup** is
passed:

- &1 -> **orcl_backup**
- &1.1 -> **orcl_backup1**
- &1..1 -> **orcl_backup.1**

Stored scripts with substitution variables must be provided with example
values at create time. These values can be provided explicitly with the
USING clause when starting RMAN or they can be entered when
prompted.

Create a Local Stored Script

After starting RMAN, connect to the target database as TARGET, and connect to a recovery catalog. The following steps create a stored script called full_backup and then run it:

```
RMAN> CONNECT TARGET SYS@oraprod

target database Password: [password]
connected to target database: PROD (DBID=38752058)

RMAN> CONNECT CATALOG recodude@catdb

recovery catalog database Password: [password]
connected to recovery catalog database

RMAN> CREATE SCRIPT full_backup
COMMENT "Perform full backup of database and archive logs"
{
    BACKUP
      INCREMENTAL LEVEL 0 TAG full_backup
      FORMAT "/u02/backup/%U"
      DATABASE PLUS ARCHIVELOG;
}

RMAN> RUN { EXECUTE SCRIPT full_backup; }
```

Create a Global Stored Script

This example creates a global script that backs up the database and archived redo log files:

```
RMAN> CONNECT TARGET SYS@oraprod

target database Password: [password]
connected to target database: ORAPROD (DBID=38752058)

RMAN> CONNECT CATALOG recoman@catdb

recovery catalog database Password: [password]
connected to recovery catalog database

RMAN> CREATE GLOBAL SCRIPT global_full_backup { BACKUP
DATABASE PLUS ARCHIVELOG; }
```

This script can now be accessed while connected to a different database:

```
RMAN> CONNECT TARGET SYS@oradev

target database Password: [password]
connected to target database: ORADEV (DBID=39823641)

RMAN> CONNECT CATALOG recoman@catdb

recovery catalog database Password: [password]
connected to recovery catalog database

RMAN> RUN { EXECUTE SCRIPT global_full_backup; }
```

Create a Stored Script with Substitution Variables

The following example connects creates a backup script that includes
three substitution variables. As the last step in creating the script, RMAN
prompts for initial values for the substitution variables.

```
RMAN> CONNECT TARGET /
RMAN> CONNECT CATALOG recoman@catdb

recovery catalog database Password: [password]
connected to recovery catalog database

RMAN> CREATE SCRIPT datafile_backup
2> { BACKUP DATAFILE &1 TAG &2 FORMAT '/u01/&3_%U'; }
Enter value for 1: 1

Enter value for 2: dfile1_bkup

Enter value for 3: dfile1

created script datafile_backup
```

When the script is executed, it is possible to pass different values to it:

```
RMAN> RUN { EXECUTE SCRIPT backup_df USING 2 dfile2_bkup
dfile2; }
```

After the values are substituted, the script executes as follows:

```
BACKUP DATAFILE 2 TAG dfile2_bkup FORMAT '/u01/dfile2_%U';
```

Deleting a stored script

You can delete stored scripts with the DELETE SCRIPT command. The following example deletes the global script named global_full_backup:

```
RMAN> DELETE GLOBAL SCRIPT global_full_backup;

deleted global script: global_full_backup
```

Replacing an Existing Script

You can overwrite an existing stored script using the REPLACE SCRIPT command. The following example shows how to replace an existing script:

```
RMAN> CONNECT TARGET SYS@oraprod

target database Password: [password]
connected to target database: ORAPROD (DBID=38752058)

RMAN> CONNECT CATALOG recoman@catdb

recovery catalog database Password: [password]
connected to recovery catalog database

RMAN> CREATE SCRIPT full_backup
COMMENT "Perform full backup of database and archive logs"
{
    BACKUP
      INCREMENTAL LEVEL 0 TAG full_backup
      FORMAT "/u02/backup/%U"
      DATABASE;
}
```

The LIST SCRIPT NAMES command will list all scripts known to the recovery catalog:

```
RMAN> LIST SCRIPT NAMES;

List of Stored Scripts in Recovery Catalog


    Scripts of Target Database ORAPROD


      Script Name
```

```
Description
--------------------------------------------------
full_backup
Perform full backup of database and archive logs

datafile_backup
```

However -- the script description is incorrect. As created, it does not back up the archive logs. You can replace the script with the following command:

```
RMAN> REPLACE SCRIPT full_backup
COMMENT "Perform full backup of database and archive logs"
{
    BACKUP
       INCREMENTAL LEVEL 0 TAG full_backup
       FORMAT "/u02/backup/%U"
       DATABASE PLUS ARCHIVELOG;
}
replaced script full_backup
```

Note that if you are replacing a Global script, you must use the REPLACE GLOBAL SCRIPT command.

Viewing stored scripts

The PRINT SCRIPT command allows you to see what actions are performed by a stored script:

```
RMAN> PRINT SCRIPT full_backup;

printing stored script: full_backup
 { BACKUP
      INCREMENTAL LEVEL 0 TAG full_backup
      FORMAT "/u02/backup/%U"
      DATABASE PLUS ARCHIVELOG;
 }
```

Back up the recovery catalog

When creating a backup strategy, you must be sure that backing up the recovery catalog database is included. If a hardware failure destroys the database holding your recovery catalog, then this will lose the metadata for all of your target databases. This will make any recovery of those databases more difficult. The recovery catalog database should be backed up as often as the target databases. As a general rule, the recovery catalog should be backed up on the same schedule as your target databases and after the last has completed. For example, if you have three databases being backed up each week, one each Thursday, Friday, and Saturday, then back up the recovery catalog database on Sunday. Having a backup of the recovery catalog will be useful in a disaster recovery scenario. In a situation where you have to restore the recovery catalog database, the record of backups in the restored recovery catalog database will allow you to restore any of the three target databases.

RMAN can be used to make the backups for the recovery catalog database. However, since you will be backing up the catalog itself, start RMAN with the NOCATALOG option so that RMAN will use the control file of the catalog database for the metadata repository. The following guidelines should be used for a recovery catalog backup strategy:

- The recovery catalog database should always be run in ARCHIVELOG mode.
- The retention policy should be set to a REDUNDANCY value greater than 1.
- Use two separate media to back up the database (i.e. disk and tape).
- Execute BACKUP DATABASE PLUS ARCHIVELOG at regular intervals.
- Use the control file rather than another recovery catalog as the metadata repository.
- Configure the control file autobackup feature to ON.

Create and use a virtual private catalog

A virtual private catalog is a set of synonyms and views that enable user access to a subset of the base recovery catalog. Prior to 11G access to the RMAN recovery catalog was an all-or-nothing proposition. Now it's possible to grant catalog access for a specific subset of databases to a given user. The owner of the base recovery catalog can GRANT or REVOKE restricted access to the catalog. Each VPC user has full read/write access to the metadata in the virtual private catalog granted to them. The RMAN metadata is stored in the schema of the virtual private catalog owner. Virtual catalog users cannot modify global RMAN scripts, although they can execute them.

Steps in creating a Virtual Private Catalog

Creating a virtual private catalog for a database user involves four steps from three locations. The first two steps are from the SQL*Plus as a user with admin privileges. The third step is executed from RMAN as the base catalog owner. The fourth step is executed from RMAN as the virtual private catalog user. The four steps are:

1. Create the VPC User.
2. Grant recovery_catalog_owner to the VPC user.
3. Grant the catalog to the new VPC user.
4. Create the virtual catalog.

From SQL*Plus, connected to the base recovery catalog database with administrator privileges:

```
SQL> CREATE USER vpc1 IDENTIFIED BY password
2 DEFAULT TABLESPACE vpcusers
3 QUOTA UNLIMITED ON vpcusers;
SQL> GRANT recovery_catalog_owner TO vpc1;
SQL> EXIT
```

From RMAN, connected to the recovery catalog database as the catalog owner catowner:

```
RMAN> CONNECT CATALOG catowner@catdb
recovery catalog database Password: password
connected to recovery catalog database
RMAN> GRANT CATALOG FOR DATABASE prod1 TO vpc1;
RMAN> EXIT;
```

From RMAN connected to the recovery catalog database as the virtual private catalog owner:

```
RMAN> CONNECT CATALOG vpc1@catdb
recovery catalog database Password: password
connected to recovery catalog database
RMAN> CREATE VIRTUAL CATALOG;
RMAN> EXIT;
```

Configuring Backup Specifications

Configure backup settings

RMAN has a number of different settings to control the specific actions taken during backups. The default settings for most of these parameters make sense for performing standard backup and recovery operations. Understanding what these parameters are will allow you to optimize the behavior for a given database. Persistent settings can be set for each target database, such as backup destinations, device type, and retention policy. The two commands of interest for this purpose are:

- **SHOW** -- This command displays the current value of settings configured for RMAN in the target database. The command will indicate whether or not the current values are set to their default. This information is also available in the V$RMAN_CONFIGURATION view.

- **CONFIGURE** -- This command allows you to change RMAN current behavior for your backup and recovery environment. If used with the keyword CLEAR, this command will reset the parameter to the default RMAN value. Some examples of the options that can be set follow:

Set the backup retention policy

The following command sets the backup retention policy to maintain three full or level 0 backups of each data file and control file. Any backups older than the third file are considered obsolete. The default value is 1.

```
CONFIGURE RETENTION POLICY TO REDUNDANCY 3;
```

Alternately, the retention policy can be given a recovery window that ensures sufficient backups are kept to recover the database to any point in time back to the supplied value:

```
CONFIGURE RETENTION POLICY TO RECOVERY WINDOW OF 7 DAYS;
```

Set the default device type

When a destination device type is not specific for a backup, RMAN sends it to whatever device type is configured as the default. RMAN is preset to use disk as the default device type. The following command allows you to change the default device type to tape:

```
CONFIGURE DEFAULT DEVICE TYPE TO sbt;
```

Regardless of the default device type, you can specifically direct a backup to a specific device type using the DEVICE TYPE clause of the BACKUP command, as shown in the following examples:

```
BACKUP DEVICE TYPE SBT DATABASE;
BACKUP DEVICE TYPE DISK DATABASE;
```

Set the default backup type

When backing up to disk, RMAN can be configured to create either backup sets or image copies by default (the backup type for tape can <u>only</u> be a backup set). In addition, RMAN can create backup sets using binary compression. Specifying the COMPRESSED option in the BACKUP TYPE TO ... BACKUPSET clause configures RMAN to use compressed backup sets by default for a given device type. Omitting the COMPRESSED keyword, disables compression. The preconfigured backup type for disk is an uncompressed backup set. The following examples show configuring RMAN backups to copies and backup sets:

```
CONFIGURE DEVICE TYPE DISK BACKUP TYPE TO BACKUPSET;
CONFIGURE DEVICE TYPE DISK BACKUP TYPE TO COPY;
```

To enable compression on backupsets, you would add the COMPRESSED keyword:

```
CONFIGURE DEVICE TYPE DISK BACKUP TYPE TO COMPRESSED BACKUPSET;
CONFIGURE DEVICE TYPE SBT BACKUP TYPE TO COMPRESSED BACKUPSET;
```

Configuring Channels

An RMAN channel is a connection to a database server session. The CONFIGURE CHANNEL command is used to configure options for disk or SBT channels. When the CONFIGURE CHANNEL command is used to specify default channel settings for a device, any previous settings are lost. Any settings not specified in the CONFIGURE CHANNEL command will be returned to their default value.

```
CONFIGURE CHANNEL DEVICE TYPE DISK MAXPIECESIZE 1G;
CONFIGURE CHANNEL DEVICE TYPE DISK FORMAT /tmp/%U;
```

Configuring Channels for Disk

RMAN allocates a single disk channel for all operations by default. You can change the default location and format for the file name for that channel. Be aware that when an explicit format is configured for disk channels, RMAN does not create backups by default in the fast recovery area.

```
CONFIGURE CHANNEL DEVICE TYPE DISK FORMAT '/u01/ora_df%t_s%s_s%p';
CONFIGURE CHANNEL DEVICE TYPE DISK FORMAT '+dgroup1';
```

Set the parallelism for a device

When multiple channels are available, RMAN can read or write in parallel. The number of channels should normally match the number of devices available (i.e. three tape drives = three channels). Allocating multiple channels for a single device can negatively affect performance unless your disk subsystem is optimized for multiple channels. The channel parallelism can be set for each device type as follows.

```
CONFIGURE DEVICE TYPE SBT PARALLELISM 2;
```

The command above only affects the parallelism for tape devices and does not alter the values of other device settings not specified.

Configure Control File and Server Parameter File Autobackups

RMAN can be set to automatically back up the control file and server parameter file whenever a backup record is added. In addition, if the database structure metadata in the control file changes and the database is in ARCHIVELOG mode, an autobackup will be taken. Control file autobackup adds additional redundancy to the recovery strategy, allowing RMAN to recover the database even after the loss of the current control file, recovery catalog, and server parameter file. The autobackup feature is enabled and disabled as follows:

```
CONFIGURE CONTROLFILE AUTOBACKUP ON;
CONFIGURE CONTROLFILE AUTOBACKUP OFF;
```

Resetting default values

The RMAN configuration settings can be returned to their default values by using the CLEAR keyword:

```
CONFIGURE DEFAULT DEVICE TYPE CLEAR;
CONFIGURE RETENTION POLICY CLEAR;
CONFIGURE CONTROLFILE AUTOBACKUP CLEAR;
```

Allocate channels to use in backing up

A channel is a connection between RMAN and a database instance. Channels specified via the CONFIGURE command will be allocated automatically. You can also allocate channels by using ALLOCATE CHANNEL within a RUN block. If ALLOCATE CHANNEL is not specified for a given job, then automatic channels will be applied. It is possible to allocate up to 255 channels and each channel can read up to 64 files in parallel. When multiple channels are allocated to a job, RMAN can read or write multiple backup sets or disk copies in parallel. Each channel operates on a single backup set or image copy at a time. When the job is complete, RMAN will release the channel. The basic guidelines for channels are:

- **DISK** -- You should allocate one channel for each output device. If the backup is being written to a striped file system or an ASM disk group, allocating multiple channels can improve performance.

- **TAPE** -- The number of tape channels should equal the number of tape devices divided by the number of duplexed copies.

Manually Allocating a Channel for a Backup

This example allocates a single tape channel for a whole database and archived redo log backup. The PARMS parameter specifies the Tivoli Storage Manager media family.

```
RUN
{
  ALLOCATE CHANNEL c1 DEVICE TYPE sbt
    PARMS 'ENV=(TDPO_OPTFILE=/opt/tsm/oracle/tdpo.opt)';
  BACKUP DATABASE;
  BACKUP ARCHIVELOG ALL NOT BACKED UP;
}
```

Distributing a Backup Across Multiple Disks

It is possible to spread a backup across multiple hard drives. You must allocate a channel of DEVICE TYPE DISK for each disk drive and specify the format string.

```
RUN
{
  ALLOCATE CHANNEL U01 DEVICE TYPE DISK FORMAT '/u01/%U';
  ALLOCATE CHANNEL U02 DEVICE TYPE DISK FORMAT '/u02/%U';
  BACKUP DATABASE PLUS ARCHIVELOG;
}
```

Configure backup optimization

When RMAN backup optimization is enabled, RMAN will skip files during a backup operation if the identical file has already been backed up to the currently specified device type. In order to determine of the file is truly identical, RMAN uses the following criteria:

- **Datafile** --The datafile must have the same DBID, checkpoint SCN, creation SCN, and RESETLOGS SCN and time as a datafile already in a backup. The datafile must be offline-normal, read-only, or closed normally.
- **Archived log** -- The log must have the same DBID, thread, sequence number, and RESETLOGS SCN and time
- **Backup set** -- The backup set must have the same DBID, backup set record ID, and stamp.

Even if RMAN determines that the file is identical to one that has already been backed up, the retention policy or the backup duplexing feature may require it to be backed up. Also, if the TO DESTINATION is used in conjunction with BACKUP RECOVERY AREA or BACKUP RECOVERY FILES, RMAN will only look for identical backups in the specific TO DESTINATION location provided. Backup optimization is enabled by issuing the following command:

```
CONFIGURE BACKUP OPTIMIZATION ON;
```

Once backup optimization has been configured for a target database, if none of the backed-up files specified for a given job has changed since the last backup, then RMAN will not back up the files again. Even if every file for a given backup is skipped because the files have already been backed up, no error will occur. Backup optimization can be overridden by including the FORCE keyword in the BACKUP command:

```
BACKUP DATABASE FORCE;
BACKUP ARCHIVELOG ALL FORCE;
```

Using RMAN to Create Backups

Create image file backups

When RMAN creates image copies, the result is bit-for-bit copies of each data file, archived redo log file, or control file. Images copies can be used as-is to perform recovery. They are generated with the RMAN BACKUP AS COPY command, an operating system command such as the UNIX cp, or by the Oracle archiver process. The default RMAN backup type can be set to image using the CONFIGURE DEVICE TYPE COMMAND:

```
CONFIGURE DEVICE TYPE DISK BACKUP TYPE TO COPY;
```

It is also possible to override the default with the AS COPY clause of the BACKUP command:

```
BACKUP AS COPY
  DEVICE TYPE DISK
  DATABASE;
```

The other format type is backup sets. Backup sets consist of one or more data files, control files, server parameter files, and archived redo log files. Each backup set consists of one or more binary files. Each binary file is called a backup piece. Backup pieces are written in a proprietary format that can only be created or restored by RMAN. The contents of a backup set are divided among multiple backup pieces only if the backup piece size is limited using MAXPIECESIZE. This keyword is an option of the ALLOCATE CHANNEL or CONFIGURE CHANNEL command. As with image copies, the default type is set with the CONFIGURE DEVICE TYPE command:

```
CONFIGURE DEVICE TYPE DISK BACKUP TYPE TO BACKUPSET;
```

The default can be overridden using the AS BACKUPSET clause. You can allow backup sets to be created on the configured default device, or direct them specifically to disk or tape.

```
BACKUP AS BACKUPSET
  DATABASE;

BACKUP AS BACKUPSET
  DEVICE TYPE DISK
  DATABASE;
```

Create a whole database backup

A whole database backup includes a backup of the control file and all data files that belong to a database. A whole database backup can be made with the database mounted or open. The RMAN command BACKUP DATABASE is used to perform a whole database backup.

```
BACKUP DATABASE;
```

Adding the PLUS ARCHIVELOGS clause will back up the database, switch the online redo logs, and include archived logs in the backup. This guarantees that you have the full set of archived logs through the time of the backup and guarantees that you can perform media recovery after restoring this backup.

```
BACKUP DATABASE PLUS ARCHIVELOG;
```

Enable fast incremental backup

The block change tracking feature improves backup performance for incremental backups by recording changed blocks for each data file. If block change tracking is enabled, RMAN uses a block change tracking file to identify changed blocks during incremental backups. This file keeps RMAN from having to scan every block in the data file that it is backing up. Block change tracking is disabled by default. A single block change tracking file is created for the whole database. By default, the change tracking file is created as an Oracle managed file in the destination specified by the DB_CREATE_FILE_DEST initialization parameter.

To enable block change tracking, execute the following ALTER DATABASE statement:

```
ALTER DATABASE ENABLE BLOCK CHANGE TRACKING;
```

You can also create the change tracking file in a specific location:

```
ALTER DATABASE ENABLE BLOCK CHANGE TRACKING
USING FILE '/ocpdir/rman_change_track.f' REUSE;
```

You can disable block change tracking by executing the following command:

```
ALTER DATABASE DISABLE BLOCK CHANGE TRACKING;
```

The V$BLOCK_CHANGE_TRACKING view can be used to determine whether change tracking is enabled, and the file name of the block change tracking file.

```
SELECT status, filename
FROM    v$block_change_tracking;

STATUS    FILENAME
--------  --------------------------------------------------
ENABLED   /u01/ocp/RDBMS/changetracking/e1_cs_2e61nr6j_.chg
```

Create duplex backup and back up backup sets

RMAN has the ability to create up to four duplexed copies when creating a backup set. Duplexing is not possible when making image copies. Duplexing is enabled using the COPIES parameter in the CONFIGURE, SET, or BACKUP commands. When duplexing, RMAN produces a single backup set with a unique key, and generates the requested number of identical copies of each backup piece in the set. It is possible to duplex backups to either disk or tape, but not to tape and disk simultaneously. The FORMAT parameter of the BACKUP command sets the destinations for the backup sets. The number of copies should never exceed the number of available tape devices when backup up to tape. Duplexing backup sets to the fast recovery area is not possible. The following command creates two backup set copies of data file 3:

```
BACKUP DEVICE TYPE DISK COPIES 2 DATAFILE 3
  FORMAT '/u01/%U','/u02/%U';
```

It is also possible to use CONFIGURE BACKUP COPIES to enable duplexing
by default. The default setting will apply to all backup sets except control
file autobackups and backupsets that are backed up using the BACKUP
BACKUPSET command. By default, CONFIGURE ... BACKUP COPIES is set to
1 for disk and tape. The following example sets duplexing for datafiles and
archivelog files on disk to two.

```
CONFIGURE CHANNEL DEVICE TYPE DISK FORMAT '/u01/%U',
'/u02/%U';
CONFIGURE DATAFILE BACKUP COPIES FOR DEVICE TYPE DISK TO 2;
CONFIGURE ARCHIVELOG BACKUP COPIES FOR DEVICE TYPE DISK TO 2;
```

Given the above configuration, the following command backs up the
database and archived logs to disk, making two copies of each data file
and archived log, placing one copy of the backup sets produced in the
/u01 directory and the other in the /u02 directory:

```
BACKUP DEVICE TYPE DISK AS BACKUPSET DATABASE PLUS
ARCHIVELOG;;
```

Backups of Backup Sets

You can use RMAN to make copies of existing previously created backup
sets with the BACKUP BACKUPSET command. This will back up backup sets
that were created on disk and can be used to spread backups among
multiple media. If RMAN determines that a backup set is corrupted or
missing, it will search for other copies of the same backup set. The
following example backs up existing backup sets to tape to ensure that all
your backups exist on both media types.

```
BACKUP DEVICE TYPE DISK AS BACKUPSET
   DATABASE PLUS ARCHIVELOG;
BACKUP
   DEVICE TYPE sbt
   BACKUPSET ALL;
```

The BACKUP BACKUPSET can also be used to manage backup space
allocation. The following backs up backup sets that were created more

than 14 days ago from disk to tape, and then deletes the backup sets from disk. If a backup was duplexed to multiple locations on disk, RMAN will delete all copies of the pieces in the backup set.

```
BACKUP
  DEVICE TYPE SBT
  BACKUPSET COMPLETED BEFORE 'SYSDATE-14'
  DELETE INPUT;
```

Create an archival backup for long-term retention

The RMAN KEEP option specifies that a backup be created as an archival backup. An archival backup is a self-contained backup that is exempt from the configured retention policy. Archival backups contain all of the files necessary to restore the backup and recover it to a consistent state. If the database is open at the time an archival backup is created, RMAN automatically generates and backs up the redo logs needed to make the backup consistent. When available, RMAN will use archival backups for disaster recovery restore operations. However, their intended purpose is to produce a snapshot of the database that can be restored on another system for testing or historical usage.

KEEP

When computing the retention policy RMAN does not consider backup pieces with the KEEP option. The KEEP option cannot be used to override the retention policy for files stored in the flash recovery area. When KEEP is specified, RMAN backs up datafiles, archived redo logs, the control file, and the server parameter file. A recovery catalog is required when KEEP FOREVER is specified because the backup records will eventually age out of the control file.

UNTIL TIME 'date_string'

This clause specifies an end date for retaining the RMAN backup or copy. After this date the backup is obsolete, regardless of the backup retention policy settings. It's possible to provide a specific date/time by using the current NLS_DATE_FORMAT, or a SQL date expression such as

'SYSDATE+90'. If a KEEP TIME is provided with a date only, then the backup becomes obsolete one second after midnight on that date.

RESTORE POINT restore_point_name

Creates a restore point matching the SCN to which RMAN must recover the backup to a consistent state. The name provided must not already exist. RMAN captures the SCN immediately after the datafile backups complete. The restore point acts as a label for the SCN to which this archival backup can be restored.

NOKEEP

This option indicates that any KEEP attributes no longer apply to the backup. After specifying NOKEEP, the backup is subject to the configured backup retention

Create a multisection, compressed and encrypted backup

Multisection backups enable RMAN channels to back up a single large file in parallel. The work is divided among multiple channels, with each channel backing up one file section in a file. This can improve the performance of backups of large datafiles. Multisection backups are enabled by specifying the SECTION SIZE parameter on the BACKUP command. Each file section is a contiguous range of blocks in a file. The SECTION SIZE parameter cannot be used in conjunction with MAXPIECESIZE. If the value of SECTION SIZE is larger than the file size, then RMAN will not use multisection backup for the file. If the section size would result in more than 256 file sections, then RMAN will increase the section size so that the result is exactly 256 sections. In the following example, the TOOLS tablespace contains a single datafile of 1 GB. The environment has two tape drives with channels allocated and the parallelism for SBT is set to two. The following command will break the tablespace datafile into two file 500MB file sections:

```
BACKUP
  SECTION SIZE 500M
  TABLESPACE tools;
```

Compressed Backups

For any use of the BACKUP command that creates backup sets, you can enable binary compression of backup sets by adding the AS COMPRESSED BACKUPSET option to the BACKUP command. RMAN will compress the backup set contents before writing to disk. Information regarding the binary compression level used is automatically recorded in the backup set. When recovering, there is no need to explicitly mention the type of compression used or how to decompress. Note that binary compression imposes a performance overhead during backup and restore operations. It consumes CPU resources, so compressed backups should not be scheduled when CPU usage is high. An example of a command to make a compressed backup is:

```
BACKUP
AS COMPRESSED BACKUPSET
DATABASE PLUS ARCHIVELOG;
```

Report on and maintain backups

A repository of RMAN metadata is always stored in the control file of each database on which it performs backup operations. In addition, a recovery catalog can be used to store metadata. When utilized, RMAN can store metadata for multiple target databases in a set of tables in a separate recovery catalog database. The LIST and REPORT commands provide several a number of reports to aid in determining backup actions that have been (or should be) performed..

RMAN LIST Command

The LIST command uses the information in the RMAN repository to provide lists of backups and other objects relating to backup and recovery.

- **LIST BACKUP** -- Allows you to list all backup sets, copies, and proxy copies of a database, tablespace, datafile, archived redo log, control file, or server parameter file.
- **LIST COPY** -- Allows you to list datafile copies and archived redo log files. By default, LIST COPY displays copies of all database files and archived redo logs.
- **LIST ARCHIVELOG** -- Allows you to list archive redo log files. You can list all archive log redo log files or you specify individual archive log files through SCN, time, or sequence number ranges.
- **LIST INCARNATION** -- Allows you to list all incarnations of a database. A new database incarnation is created when you open with the RESETLOGS option.
- **LIST DB_UNIQUE_NAME** -- In a Data Guard environment, each database is distinguished by its DB_UNIQUE_NAME initialization parameter setting. You can list all databases that have the same DBID.
- **LIST ... FOR DB_UNIQUE_NAME** -- Allows you to list all backups and copies for a specified database in a Data Guard environment or for all databases in the environment.
- **LIST RESTORE POINT** -- Allows you to list restore points known to the RMAN repository.
- **LIST SCRIPT NAMES** -- Allows you to list the names of recovery catalog scripts created with the CREATE SCRIPT or REPLACE SCRIPT command.
- **LIST FAILURE** -- A failure is a persistent data corruption mapped to a repair option.

List has a number of options that enables you to control how output is displayed. Some of the most common LIST options are:

- **LIST EXPIRED** -- Lists backups or copies that are recorded in the RMAN repository but that were not present at the expected location on disk or tape during the most recent crosscheck.

- **LIST ... BY FILE** -- Lists backups of each datafile, archived redo log file, control file, and server parameter file. Each row describes a backup of a file.
- **LIST ... SUMMARY** -- Provides a one-line summary of each backup.

RMAN REPORT Command

The RMAN REPORT command performs an analysis of the available backups and your database. The results of this can be used to determine actions that you should take, such as backing up specific files or removing obsolete backups to free up disk space. Some of the common uses of the REPORT command are:

- **REPORT NEED BACKUP** -- Reports which database files need to be backed up to meet a configured or specified retention policy.
- **REPORT UNRECOVERABLE** -- Reports which database files require backup because they have been affected by some NOLOGGING operation such as a direct-path INSERT.
- **REPORT OBSOLETE** -- Returns full backups, datafile copies, and archived redo logs recorded in the RMAN repository that can be deleted because they are no longer required.
- **REPORT SCHEMA** -- Returns the names of all datafiles and tablespaces for the target database at the specified point in time.

Performing User-Managed Backup and Recovery

Recover from a lost TEMP file

If one of more files belonging to the temporary tablespace is lost, any SQL statements that require space in the temporary tablespace will generate an error. If the database is up and you would like to recreate the file immediately, you can do so by creating a new datafile and dropping the old one as follows:

```
SQL> ALTER TABLESPACE temp ADD TEMPFILE
'/u01/app/oracle/oradata/orcl/temp02.dbf' SIZE 50M;
SQL> ALTER TABLESPACE temp DROP TEMPFILE
'/u01/app/oracle/oradata/orcl/temp01.dbf';
```

If the loss or damage to the datafile occurred while the database is down, simply starting the instance will automatically recreate the datafile. If Oracle detects a missing datafile on startup, it will issue the commands to recreate it. You will see a message in the alert log such are:

```
Re-creating tempfile /u01/app/oracle/oradata/orcl/temp01.dbf
```

If the file damage occurred while the database is started, but you would prefer to have the recovery done automatically (and assuming that restarting the database is an option), then shutting down and restarting the instance will recreate the file.

Recover from a lost redo log group

If all members of an online redo log group are damaged, the recovery process depends on the type of online redo log group affected and the whether or not the database is in archivelog mode. If the damaged online redo log group is current and active, then it is needed for crash recovery; otherwise, it is not. You can determine the status of the group associated with the damage files from V$LOGFILE:

```
SELECT group#, status, member
FROM   v$logfile;

GROUP#     STATUS          MEMBER
-------    -----------     ---------------------
0001                       /oracle/dbs/log1a.f
0001                       /oracle/dbs/log1b.f
0002       INVALID         /oracle/dbs/log2a.f
0002       INVALID         /oracle/dbs/log2b.f
0003                       /oracle/dbs/log3a.f
0003                       /oracle/dbs/log3b.f
```

You can determine which groups are active from the V$LOG view:

```
SELECT group#, status, archived
FROM   v$log;

GROUP#  STATUS      ARCHIVED
------  ---------   -----------
 0001   INACTIVE    YES
 0002   ACTIVE      NO
 0003   CURRENT     NO
```

If all members of an inactive online redo log group are damaged, then the procedure depends on whether it is possible to repair the media problem that damaged the group. If the failure is transient, then fix the problem. The log writer will reuse the redo log group when required. For permanent failures, the damaged redo log group will halt normal database operation when the database tries to use it. The damaged group must be reinitialized manually by issuing the ALTER DATABASE CLEAR LOGFILE statement.

If all members of an active (but not current) log group are damaged and the database is still running, issue the ALTER SYSTEM CHECKPOINT statement. If the checkpoint is successful, then the redo log group will become inactive. At this point you can follow the steps for an inactive online redo log group. If the checkpoint is unsuccessful, or the database has halted, then depending on the archiving mode you must follow the recovery procedures corresponding to the current log group.

The current log group is the one LGWR is currently writing to. If a LGWR I/O operation fails, then LGWR terminates and the instance is terminated. In this case, you must restore a backup, perform incomplete recovery, and open the database with the RESETLOGS option.

Recovering from the Loss of Active Logs in NOARCHIVELOG Mode

If the media failure is temporary, then correct the problem so that the database can reuse the group when required.

- Restore the database from a consistent, whole database backup (data files and control files).

- Mount the database:

- To allow the database to reset the online redo logs, you must first mimic incomplete recovery:

```
RECOVER DATABASE UNTIL CANCEL
CANCEL
```
- Open the database using the RESETLOGS option:

```
ALTER DATABASE OPEN RESETLOGS;
```
- Shut down the database consistently.

```
SHUTDOWN IMMEDIATE
```
- Make a whole database backup.

Recovering from Loss of Active Logs in ARCHIVELOG Mode

- Begin incomplete media recovery, recovering up through the log before the damaged log.

- Ensure that the current name of the lost redo log can be used for a newly created file. If not, then rename the members of the damaged online redo log group to a new location.

- Open the database using the RESETLOGS option:

```
ALTER DATABASE OPEN RESETLOGS;
```

Recover from the loss of password file

If the Oracle password file is lost or damaged, it must be recreated using the orapwd command-line utility. When a new password file is created, orapwd prompts for the SYS password and stores the result in the created password file. The syntax of the ORAPWD command is as follows:

```
ORAPWD FILE=filename [ENTRIES=numusers] [FORCE={Y|N}]
[IGNORECASE={Y|N}]
```

The command arguments of orapwd follow. for all parameters, there are no spaces permitted around the equal sign (=) character.

- **FILE** --Name to assign to the password file. You must supply a complete path. If you supply only a file name, the file is written to the current directory.
- **ENTRIES** -- Maximum number of entries (user accounts) to permit in the file. This is optional.
- **FORCE** -- If Y, permits overwriting an existing password file. This is optional.
- **IGNORECASE** -- If Y, passwords are treated as case-insensitive. This is optional.

The following command creates a password file named orapworcl that allows up to 30 privileged users with different passwords.

```
orapwd FILE=orapworcl ENTRIES=30
```

Perform user-managed complete database recovery

Complete database recovery is normally performed when one or more datafiles become damaged or lost. In a complete database recovery, all available redo logs will be applied to recover the database to the current SCN. The following recovery makes these assumptions:

- The current control file is available.
- You have backups of all needed data files.
- All necessary archived redo logs are available.

The basic steps to perform complete recovery while the database is not open follow. You can recover either all damaged data files in one operation or perform individual recovery of each damaged data file in separate operations.

1. If the database is open, query V$RECOVER_FILE to determine which data files must be recovered and why they must be recovered.

2. Query the V$ARCHIVED_LOG and V$RECOVERY_LOG views to determine which archived redo log files are needed.

3. If some archived logs must be restored, restore the required archived redo log files to the location specified by LOG_ARCHIVE_DEST_1.

4. If the database is open, then shut it down.

5. If the files are permanently damaged, then identify the most recent backups for the damaged files. Restore only the data files damaged by the media failure: do not restore undamaged data files or any online redo log files.

6. Use an operating system utility to restore the data files to their default location or to a new location if there is a media failure that cannot be fixed.

7. Connect to the database with administrator privileges. Then start a new instance and mount, but do not open, the database.

8. If you restored one or more damaged data files to alternative locations, then update the control file of the database to reflect the new data file names.

9. Issue a statement to recover the database, tablespace, or data file. For example, enter one of the following RECOVER commands:

```
RECOVER AUTOMATIC DATABASE
RECOVER AUTOMATIC TABLESPACE users
RECOVER AUTOMATIC DATAFILE
'?/oradata/trgt/users01.dbf'
```

10. If no archived redo logs are required for complete media recovery, then the database applies all necessary online redo log files and terminates recovery.

11. After recovery terminates, open the database for use:

Perform user-managed incomplete database recovery

This section describes steps to perform complete incomplete. When performing an incomplete recovery you must recover all damaged data files in a single operation.

1. If the database is open, query V$RECOVER_FILE to determine which data files must be recovered and why they must be recovered.

2. Query the V$ARCHIVED_LOG and V$RECOVERY_LOG views to determine which archived redo log files are needed.

3. If some archived logs must be restored, restore the required archived redo log files to the location specified by LOG_ARCHIVE_DEST_1.

4. If the database is open, then shut it down.

5. If the files are permanently damaged, then identify the most recent backups for the damaged files. Restore only the data files damaged by the media failure: do not restore undamaged data files or any online redo log files.

6. Use an operating system utility to restore the data files to their default location or to a new location if there is a media failure that cannot be fixed.

7. Connect to the database with administrator privileges. Then start a new instance and mount, but do not open, the database.

8. If you restored one or more damaged data files to alternative locations, then update the control file of the database to reflect the new data file names.

9. Begin cancel-based recovery by issuing the following command in SQL*Plus:

```
RECOVER DATABASE UNTIL CANCEL
```

10. Continue applying redo log files until the last log has been applied to the restored data files, then cancel recovery by executing the following command:

```
CANCEL
```

11. Open the database with the RESETLOGS option. You must always reset the logs after incomplete recovery or recovery with a backup control file.

12. After opening the database with the RESETLOGS option, check the alert log to determine whether the database detected inconsistencies between the data dictionary and the control file.

Perform user-managed and server managed backups

A user-managed backup and recovery strategy is one that does not depend on using Recovery Manager. When performing user-managed backups, a significant number of activities that RMAN performs automatically must instead be performed manually. Before starting the backup, you can use the Oracle data dictionary views to obtain information about the database needed for backup.

Query the V$DATAFILE and V$CONTROLFILE views to identify the data files and control files for your database.

```
SELECT    t.name AS TABLESPACE, f.name AS DATAFILE
FROM      v$tablespace t
          INNER JOIN v$datafile f
          ON t.ts# = f.ts#
ORDER BY t.name;

SELECT name
FROM    v$controlfile;
```

Query the V$BACKUP view to check whether a data file is part of a current online tablespace backup.

```
SELECT t.name AS TB_NAME, d.file# as DF#, d.name AS DF_NAME,
b.status
FROM    v$datafile d
        INNER JOIN v$tablespace t
        ON d.ts#=t.ts#
        INNER JOIN v$backup b
        ON b.file#=d.file#
WHERE   b.status='ACTIVE';
```

If the database has been shut down with the NORMAL, IMMEDIATE, or TRANSACTIONAL options, then it is in a consistent state and you can create a usable backup by copying all of the data files with operating system commands. If the database is open, has just had an instance failure or been SHUTDOWN with the ABORT option, the database is in an inconsistent state. Copying the files at this time will create a backup that is inconsistent with the database SCN. Backups taken for a database in NOARCHIVELOG mode must be consistent. When a database is in ARCHIVELOG mode, it is possible to take inconsistent backups because the archived logs can be used to apply recovery to the datafiles to bring them to a consistent state.

Creating a consistent whole database backup:

1. Shut down the database with the NORMAL, IMMEDIATE, or TRANSACTIONAL options.

2. Use an operating system utility to make backups of all data files, all control files, and the initialization parameter file.

3. Restart the database with the STARTUP command.

Creating an online database backup

Creating a backup of datafiles while the database is active can only be done while the database is in ARCHIVELOG mode. In addition, you must put a read/write tablespace in backup mode when the tablespace is online and the database is open. This is done with the ALTER TABLESPACE ... BEGIN BACKUP statement. When in backup mode, the database copies whole changed data blocks into the redo stream. A backup taken using this method will still require recovery to be performed on it using the archived logs.

1. Set the first tablespace to be backed up into backup mode.

2. Back up the online data files of the tablespace with operating system commands.

3. After backing up the data files of the online tablespace, run the SQL statement ALTER TABLESPACE with the END BACKUP option.

4. Repeat for all tablespaces in the database

5. Archive the unarchived redo logs so that the redo required to recover the tablespace backup is archived.

Creating a server-managed database backup

When using the RMAN utility, all of the steps above can be boiled down to a single command. The RMAN command BACKUP DATABASE is used to perform a whole database backup. I'm pretty sure this test topic was requested by Oracle's marketing department to show how wonderful RMAN is. If you have configured your RMAN defaults correctly, the process to create a server managed database backup is to issue the following command:

```
RMAN> BACKUP DATABASE;
```

Identify the need of backup mode

When performing user-managed backups of the datafiles for an online read-write tablespace while the database is open, it is required that the tablespace first be placed into backup mode. Because the tablespace is online and writable, it is possible for the database writer (DBWR) to be updating the file at the same time that the operating system utility is copying it. When this happens, it is possible for the utility to read a block in a partially-updated state. In this case, the block that is copied to the backup media would contain some newer and some older data. This type of logical corruption is known as a fractured block. Fractured blocks are not consistent with any SCN and Oracle does not normally store sufficient information to repair them.

This situation can be resolved by placing datafiles into backup mode with the ALTER DATABASE or ALTER TABLESPACE statement with the BEGIN BACKUP clause. Once a tablespace has been put into backup mode, Oracle writes the before image for an entire block to the redo stream before making changes to it. The changes made to the block are also stored in the online redo log. Backup mode also freezes the data file checkpoint until the file is removed from backup mode. During recovery, the before image can be used to repair fractured blocks.

RMAN itself does not require extra logging or backup mode because it knows the format of data blocks and will never back up fractured blocks.

RMAN also does not need to freeze the data file header checkpoint. It is aware of the order in which the blocks are read, so it can always capture a known good checkpoint.

Back up and recover a control file

The control file is critical to recovery of an Oracle database and so backing it up is of paramount importance. There are numerous ways to back up the control file. If you are using RMAN as your backup tool, the easiest of these is simply to configure RMAN to automatically back up the control file and server parameter file whenever a backup record is added. The autobackup feature is enabled and disabled as follows:

```
CONFIGURE CONTROLFILE AUTOBACKUP ON;
```

Even if CONTROLFILE AUTOBACKUP is not enabled, performing a whole database backup in RMAN will include a copy of the control file. The RMAN command BACKUP DATABASE is used to perform a whole database backup.

```
BACKUP DATABASE;
```

Outside of RMAN, there are two ALTER DATABASE commands that can be used to back up a control file. You can back up the control file to a binary file using the following statement:

```
ALTER DATABASE BACKUP CONTROLFILE TO
'/oracle/backup/control.bkp';
```

Alternately, the following command writes a SQL script to a trace file that can be used to reproduce the control file. The alert log will contain the name and location of the trace file.

```
ALTER DATABASE BACKUP CONTROLFILE TO TRACE;
```

Finally, for a user managed backup while the database is shut down, you can use operating system commands to copy the control file.

Recovering the Database with a Backup Control File

In a recovery scenario where all copies of the current control file are lost or damaged, then you must restore and mount a backup control file. Copy the backup control file to all of the locations listed in the CONTROL_FILES initialization parameter. After the files are in place, the RECOVER command must be issued, even if no datafiles have been restored.

```
RECOVER DATABASE USING BACKUP CONTROLFILE UNTIL CANCEL;
```

Once the restore operation has been completed, open the database with the RESETLOGS option.

Using RMAN to Perform Recovery

Perform complete recovery from a critical or noncritical data file loss using RMAN

The scope of 'performing a complete database recovery' is huge and depends on dozens of factors. However, the exam is not going to get into a hugely complex recovery scenario. This section makes the following assumptions:

- Some or all data files have been lost, but the database has not lost all current control files or an entire online redo log group.
- The database is using the current server parameter file.
- The complete set of archived redo logs and incremental backups needed for recovery of the data file backups are available. Every data file either has a backup, or a complete set of online and archived redo logs goes back to the creation of a data file with no backup.
- An encrypted tablespace is not part of the recovery.
- The database runs in a single-instance configuration.
- The database uses a fast recovery area.

Prior to starting the recovery, you should ideally perform all of the following steps:

- Identify the Database Files to Restore or Recover
- Determine the DBID of the Database
- Preview Backups Used in Restore Operations
- Validate Backups Before Restoring Them
- Restore Archived Redo Logs Needed for Recovery

To restore and recover the whole database:

1. Start RMAN and connect to a target database.

```
% rman
RMAN> CONNECT TARGET /
```

2. If the database is not mounted, then mount but do not open the database.

```
STARTUP MOUNT;
```

3. Use the SHOW command to see which channels are preconfigured.

```
SHOW ALL;
```

If the necessary devices and channels are already configured, then no action is necessary. Otherwise, you can use the CONFIGURE command to configure automatic channels, or include ALLOCATE CHANNEL commands within a RUN block.

4. Restore and recover the database.

```
RMAN> RESTORE DATABASE;
Starting restore at 20-JAN-13
.
.
.
Finished restore at 20-JAN-13

RMAN> RECOVER DATABASE;

Starting recover at 20-JAN-13
.
.
.
media recovery complete, elapsed time: 00:00:21
Finished recover at 20-JAN-13
```

5. Examine the output to see if media recovery was successful. If so, open the database.

```
ALTER DATABASE OPEN;
```

Perform incomplete recovery using RMAN

There are several situations where it is desirable (or necessary) to perform an incomplete recovery:

- To recover the database to an SCN before a user or administrative error.
- The database contains corrupt blocks.
- Complete database recovery is not possible because required archived redo logs are not available.
- When creating a test database or a reporting database from production database backups.

This section will list the steps for cancel-based incomplete recovery and time or SCN-based incomplete recovery. Both scenarios assume that backups of all required data files exist and the current control file is available.

To perform cancel-based recovery:

When performing a cancel-based recovery, the recovery prompts you with the suggested file names of archived redo log files. The recovery will continue until CANCEL is specified instead of a file name or when all redo has been applied to the data files.

1. If the database is open, query V$RECOVER_FILE to determine which data files must be recovered and why they must be recovered.

2. Query the V$ARCHIVED_LOG and V$RECOVERY_LOG views to determine which archived redo log files are needed. If all archived logs are available in the default location, then skip to Step 3. If some archived logs must be restored, and if sufficient space is available, then restore the required archived redo log files to the location specified by LOG_ARCHIVE_DEST_1.

3. If the database is open, then shut it down.

```
SHUTDOWN IMMEDIATE
```

4. Identify the most recent backups for the damaged files. Restore only the data files damaged by the media failure: do not restore undamaged data files or any online redo log files.

5. Use an operating system utility to restore the data files to their default location or to a new location. For example, a Linux or UNIX user restoring users01.dbf to its default location might enter:

```
% cp /backup/users01_10_24_06.dbf
$ORACLE_HOME/oradata/trgt/users01.dbf
```

6. If the files were not restored to the original location, indicate the new location of these files in the control file with the ALTER DATABASE RENAME FILE statement.

7. Connect to the database with administrator privileges. Then start a new instance and mount, but do not open, the database.

```
STARTUP MOUNT
```

8. Begin cancel-based recovery by issuing the following command in SQL*Plus:

```
RECOVER DATABASE UNTIL CANCEL
```

9. Continue applying redo log files until the last log has been applied to the restored data files, then cancel recovery by executing the following command:

```
CANCEL
```

10. Open the database with the RESETLOGS option. You must always reset the logs after incomplete recovery or recovery with a backup control file.

```
ALTER DATABASE OPEN RESETLOGS;
```

11. After opening the database with the RESETLOGS option, check the alert log. There should be a message showing the RESETLOGS was issued (i.e. 'RESETLOGS after incomplete recovery...'). Also the alert log may indicate that the database detected inconsistencies between the data dictionary and the control file

Performing Time-Based or Change-Based Incomplete Recovery

This section describes how to specify an SCN or time for the end point of recovery. If your database is affected by seasonal time changes (for example, daylight savings time), then you may experience a problem if a time appears twice in the redo log and you want to recover to the second, or later time. To handle time changes, perform cancel-based or change-based recovery.

1. If the database is open, query V$RECOVER_FILE to determine which data files must be recovered and why they must be recovered.

2. Query the V$ARCHIVED_LOG and V$RECOVERY_LOG views to determine which archived redo log files are needed. If all archived logs are available in the default location, then skip to Step 3. If some archived logs must be restored, and if sufficient space is available, then restore the required archived redo log files to the location specified by LOG_ARCHIVE_DEST_1.

3. If the database is open, then shut it down.

   ```
   SHUTDOWN IMMEDIATE
   ```
4. Identify the most recent backups for the damaged files. Restore only the data files damaged by the media failure: do not restore undamaged data files or any online redo log files.

5. Use an operating system utility to restore the data files to their default location or to a new location. For example, a Linux or UNIX user restoring users01.dbf to its default location might enter:

   ```
   % cp /backup/users01_10_24_06.dbf
   $ORACLE_HOME/oradata/trgt/users01.dbf
   ```
6. If the files were not restored to the original location, indicate the new location of these files in the control file with the ALTER DATABASE RENAME FILE statement.

7. Connect to the database with administrator privileges. Then start a new instance and mount, but do not open, the database.

```
STARTUP MOUNT
```

8. Issue the RECOVER DATABASE UNTIL statement to begin recovery. If recovering to an SCN, then specify as a decimal number without quotation marks. For example, to recover through SCN 24389 issue:

```
RECOVER DATABASE UNTIL CHANGE 24389;
```

If recovering to a time, then the time is always specified using the following format, delimited by single quotation marks: 'YYYY-MM-DD:HH24:MI:SS'.

```
RECOVER DATABASE UNTIL TIME '2013-01-20:09:23:15'
```

9. Apply the necessary redo log files to recover the restored data files. The database automatically terminates the recovery when it reaches the correct time, and returns a message indicating whether recovery is successful.

10. Open the database with the RESETLOGS option. You must always reset the logs after incomplete recovery or recovery with a backup control file.

```
ALTER DATABASE OPEN RESETLOGS;
```

11. After opening the database with the RESETLOGS option, check the alert log. There should be a message showing the RESETLOGS was issued (i.e. 'RESETLOGS after incomplete recovery...'). Also the alert log may indicate that the database detected inconsistencies between the data dictionary and the control file

Recover using incrementally updated backups

The RMAN BACKUP INCREMENTAL command creates an incremental backup of a database. Incremental backups capture block-level changes to a database made after a previous incremental backup. Recovery with incremental backups is faster than using redo logs alone. There are three types of incremental backups:

- **Level 0** -- This is the starting point for an incremental backup. It backs up all blocks in the database and is identical in content to a full backup.
- **Level 1 Differential** -- This backup contains only blocks changed since the most recent incremental backup. This is the default Level 1 backup.
- **Level 1 Cumulative** -- This backup contains only blocks changed since the most recent level 0 backup.

When restoring incremental backups, RMAN uses the level 0 backup as the starting point. It then uses the level 1 backups to update changed blocks where possible to avoid reapplying changes from redo one at a time. If incremental backups are available, then RMAN uses them during recovery.

The following example creates a level 0 incremental backup to serve as a base for an incremental backup strategy:

```
BACKUP INCREMENTAL LEVEL 0 DATABASE;
```

The following example creates a level 1 cumulative incremental backup:

```
BACKUP INCREMENTAL LEVEL 1 CUMULATIVE DATABASE;
```

The following example creates a level 1 differential incremental backup:

```
BACKUP INCREMENTAL LEVEL 1 DATABASE;
```

Switch to image copies for fast recovery

An option to reduce recovery time is to use incrementally updated backups. In this strategy, an image copy of each data file is created. Periodically the image copy is rolled forward by making and applying a level 1 incremental backup. If the image files need to be used for recovery, the only redo that needs to be applied is whatever redo has been generated since the last incremental backup.

Incrementally Updating Backups

This process avoids the overhead of making full image copy backups of datafiles, while minimizing media recovery time. If incremental changes are created and applied by a daily backup script, there will never be more than 1 day of redo to apply during media recovery. After the incremental changes have been made to a given backup data file, it will be identical to the datafile at the time of the most recently applied incremental level 1 backup.

- Create a full image copy backup of a data file with a specified tag.
- At regular intervals, make a level 1 differential incremental backup of the data file with the same tag as the base data file copy.
- Apply the incremental backup to the most recent backup with the same tag.

To create incremental backups for use in an incrementally updated backups strategy, use the BACKUP ... FOR RECOVER OF COPY WITH TAG form of the BACKUP command. The script following is a very basic example of implementing a strategy based on incrementally updated backups.

```
RUN
{
  RECOVER COPY OF DATABASE
    WITH TAG 'incr_update';
  BACKUP
    INCREMENTAL LEVEL 1
    FOR RECOVER OF COPY WITH TAG 'incr_update'
    DATABASE;
}
```

Restore a database onto a new host

Restoring a backup of your existing database to a new host might be required if your current host develops hardware troubles. Alternately, you may simply be upgrading to a newer hardware platform. In any event,

RMAN can be used to move your existing data to the new platform as follows:

1. Start RMAN and connect to a target database and recovery catalog.

2. Run a LIST command to see a listing of backups of the datafile and control file autobackups.

   ```
   LIST COPY;
   LIST BACKUP OF CONTROLFILE;
   ```

3. Copy the backups to the new host with an operating system utility.

4. Edit the /etc/group file on the new host so that you are included in the DBA group:

   ```
   dba:*:614:<your_user_name>
   ```

5. Set the ORACLE_SID environment variable on the new host to the same value used on the original:

   ```
   % setenv ORACLE_SID orclprod
   ```

6. Start RMAN on hostb and connect to the target database without connecting to the recovery catalog.

   ```
   % rman NOCATALOG
   RMAN> CONNECT TARGET /
   ```

7. Set the DBID and start the database instance without mounting the database.

   ```
   SET DBID 423498230;
   STARTUP NOMOUNT
   ```

8. RMAN will fail to find the server parameter file, which has not yet been restored, but will start the instance with a "dummy" file.

9. Allocate a channel to the media manager, then restore the server parameter file as a client-side parameter file and use the SET command to indicate the location of the autobackup.

```
RUN
{
ALLOCATE CHANNEL c1 DEVICE TYPE sbt PARMS '...';
SET CONTROLFILE AUTOBACKUP FORMAT FOR DEVICE TYPE DISK
TO '/tmp/%F';
RESTORE SPFILE
TO PFILE '?/oradata/test/inittrgta.ora'
FROM AUTOBACKUP;
SHUTDOWN ABORT;
}
```

10. Edit the restored initialization parameter file.

11. Change any location-specific parameters, for example, those ending in _DEST, to reflect the new directory structure.

```
    a.  IFILE
    b.  LOG_ARCHIVE_DEST_1
    c.  CONTROL_FILES
    d.
```

12. Restart the instance with the edited initialization parameter file.

```
STARTUP FORCE NOMOUNT
PFILE='?/oradata/test/inittrgta.ora';
```

13. Restore the control file from an autobackup and then mount the database.

```
RUN
{
ALLOCATE CHANNEL c1 DEVICE TYPE sbt PARMS '...';
RESTORE CONTROLFILE FROM AUTOBACKUP;
ALTER DATABASE MOUNT;
}
```

14. RMAN restores the control file to whatever locations you specified in the CONTROL_FILES initialization parameter.

15. Catalog the datafile copies that you moved to the new host, using their new filenames. You can use CATALOG START WITH if the files are in directories with a common prefix:

```
CATALOG START WITH '/oracle/oradata/trgt/';
```

16. If you want to specify files individually, then you can execute a CATALOG command as follows:

```
CATALOG DATAFILECOPY
'/oracle/oradata/trgt/system01.dbf',
'/oracle/oradata/trgt/undotbs01.dbf',
'/oracle/oradata/trgt/cwmlite01.dbf',
'/oracle/oradata/trgt/drsys01.dbf',
'/oracle/oradata/trgt/example01.dbf',
'/oracle/oradata/trgt/indx01.dbf',
'/oracle/oradata/trgt/tools01.dbf',
'/oracle/oradata/trgt/users01.dbf';
```

17. Start a SQL*Plus session on the new database and query the database filenames recorded in the control file.

18. Because the control file is from the hosta database, the recorded filenames use the original hosta filenames. You can query V$ views to obtain this information. Run the following query in SQL*Plus:

```
COLUMN NAME FORMAT a60
SPOOL  LOG '/tmp/db_filenames.out'
SELECT file# AS "File/Grp#", name
FROM   v$datafile
UNION
SELECT group#, member
FROM   v$logfile;
SPOOL OFF
EXIT
```

19. Write the RMAN restore and recovery script. The script must include the following steps:

- ✓ For each datafile on the destination host that is restored to a different path than it had on the source host, use a SET NEWNAME command to specify the new path on the destination host.
- ✓ For each online redo log that is to be created at a different location than it had on the source host, use SQL ALTER

DATABASE RENAME FILE commands to specify the pathname on the destination host.

✓ Perform a SET UNTIL operation to limit recovery to the end of the archived redo logs.

✓ Restore and recover the database.

✓ Run the SWITCH DATAFILE ALL command so that the control file recognizes the new datafile path names.

```
RUN
{
ALLOCATE CHANNEL c1 DEVICE TYPE sbt PARMS '...';

SET NEWNAME FOR DATAFILE 1 TO
'?/oradata/test/system01.dbf';
SET NEWNAME FOR DATAFILE 2 TO
'?/oradata/test/undotbs01.dbf';
SET NEWNAME FOR DATAFILE 3 TO
'?/oradata/test/indx01.dbf';
SET NEWNAME FOR DATAFILE 4 TO
'?/oradata/test/tools01.dbf';
SET NEWNAME FOR DATAFILE 5 TO
'?/oradata/test/users01.dbf';
SQL "ALTER DATABASE RENAME FILE
''/dev3/oracle/dbs/redo01.log''
TO ''?/oradata/test/redo01.log'' ";
SQL "ALTER DATABASE RENAME FILE
''/dev3/oracle/dbs/redo02.log''
TO ''?/oradata/test/redo02.log'' ";

SET UNTIL SCN 123456;
RESTORE DATABASE;
SWITCH DATAFILE ALL;

# recover the database
RECOVER DATABASE;
}
EXIT
```

20. Execute the script created in the previous step.

```
% rman TARGET / NOCATALOG
RMAN> @reco_test.rman
```

21. From the RMAN prompt, open the database with the RESETLOGS option:

```
ALTER DATABASE OPEN RESETLOGS;
```

Recover using a backup control file

In a recovery scenario where all copies of the current control file are lost or damaged, then you must restore and mount a backup control file. Copy the backup control file to all of the locations listed in the CONTROL_FILES initialization parameter. After the files are in place, the RECOVER command must be issued, even if no datafiles have been restored.

RMAN automatically searches during the recovery process for online and archived logs that are not recorded in the RMAN repository. Any that are found will be cataloged in the control file. It searches for archived redo logs in any current archiving destination that are in the log format specified in the initialization parameter file used to start the instance. RMAN will also attempt to locate the online redo logs by using the filenames listed in the control file. If the archiving destination or format has been altered during recovery, or if you added new online log members after the backup of the control file, this process may fail. In that case, RMAN may not be able to automatically catalog a needed online or archived log. If this happens, you must use the CATALOG command to manually add the required redo logs so that recovery can proceed.

The database will expect to find the control files in the locations defined in the CONTROL_FILES initialization parameter. If this parameter is not set, then the default control file location uses the rules defined in the CREATE CONTROLFILE statement. If the backup control files cannot be copied to the original locations, the CONTROL_FILES initialization parameter can be changed to reflect new locations.

Once the control files are in place and any required redo logs have been cataloged, you may recover the database with the RECOVER command:

```
RECOVER DATABASE USING BACKUP CONTROLFILE UNTIL CANCEL;
```

Once the restore operation has been completed, open the database with the RESETLOGS option.

Perform Disaster recovery

Disaster recovery assumes that the entire database has been lost, including all datafiles, the recovery catalog database, all current control files, all online redo log files, and all parameter files. Recovering the database in the event of a loss like this requires:

- Backups of all datafiles
- All archived redo logs generated after the creation time of the oldest backup that you intend to restore
- At least one control file autobackup
- A record of the DBID of the database

In this recovery, it is assumed that the server hardware the database was on has been damaged beyond repair. A full backup exists and the Oracle software has been installed on a new host with the same directory structure. The four requirements listed above have been met.

To recover the database on the new host:

1. If possible, restore or re-create all relevant network files such as tnsnames.ora and listener.ora and a password file.

2. Start RMAN and connect to the target database instance using operating system authentication.

   ```
   RMAN> CONNECT TARGET /
   ```

3. Specify the DBID for the target database with the SET DBID command.

   ```
   SET DBID 343487540;
   ```

4. Issue the STARTUP NOMOUNT command.

5. Allocate a channel to the media manager and then restore the server parameter file from autobackup.

```
RUN
{
ALLOCATE CHANNEL c1 DEVICE TYPE sbt;
RESTORE SPFILE FROM AUTOBACKUP;
}
```

6. Restart the instance with the restored server parameter file.

```
STARTUP FORCE NOMOUNT;
```

7. Write a command file to perform the restore and recovery operation, and then execute the command file. The command file should do the following:

   ✓ Allocate a channel to the media manager.
   ✓ Restore a control file autobackup.
   ✓ Mount the restored control file.
   ✓ Catalog any backups not recorded in the repository with the CATALOG command.
   ✓ Restore the datafiles to their original locations.
   ✓ Recover the datafiles. RMAN stops recovery when it reaches the log sequence number specified.

```
RMAN> RUN
{
ALLOCATE CHANNEL t1 DEVICE TYPE sbt;
RESTORE CONTROLFILE FROM AUTOBACKUP;
ALTER DATABASE MOUNT;
RESTORE DATABASE;
RECOVER DATABASE;
}
```

8. If recovery was successful, then open the database and reset the online logs:

```
ALTER DATABASE OPEN RESETLOGS;
```

Using RMAN to Duplicate a Database

Creating a duplicate database

The DUPLICATE command has been enhanced in 11G to allow cloning a database to a remote site directly over the network without requiring an existing backup. An ASM-to-ASM DUPLICATE over the network is also supported. There is no need to copy or move backups to the remote site before executing the DUPLICATE command. Some of the requirements for performing a DUPLICATE operation are:

- The Source database must be in MOUNT or OPEN status
- The Source and Destination databases must be on the same OS
- The Source and Destination databases must have password files with matched SYS passwords.
- The Source and Destination databases must be accessible via Oracle Net.

Filename Conversion

When duplicating a database, RMAN must generate names for the new database files. If you are performing a backup to a different host and the directory structure is exactly the same as the source host, then the exact same filenames can be used. In this case, you would specify the NOFILENAMECHECK option for the DUPLICATE command. If the directory structure is different, or if you want to name files differently, then you must specify patterns for DUPLICATE to use in renaming the files. You can rename the control files, data files, online redo log files, and tempfiles. There are DUPLICATE parameters to handle each of these.

- **db_file_name_convert** -- Allows you to set a pattern for renaming datafiles
  db_file_name_convert '/u02/app/oracle','u04/app/oracle'
- **spfile...log_file_name_convert** -- Allows you to set a pattern for renaming log files
  spfile...set log_file_name_convert '/u02/app/oracle','u04/app/oracle'

- **spfile...parameter_value_convert** -- Allows you to set a pattern conversion for all parameters with directory paths <u>except</u> database files and log files.
  spfile...parameter_value_convert
  '/u02/app/oracle','u04/app/oracle'

```
 RMAN> duplicate database to database2
2> from active database
3> db_file_name_convert '/u02/app/oracle','u04/app/oracle'
4> spfile
5> set log_file_name_convert '/u02/app/oracle',
'u04/app/oracle'
6> parameter_value_convert '/u02/app/oracle',
'u04/app/oracle';
```

Using a duplicate database

A duplicate database is a copy of a given database with a unique DBID. The duplicate is completely independent of the source database and can be registered in the same recovery catalog. As a general rule, duplicate databases are used for testing. Some of the more common uses for a duplicate database are:

- Test backup and recovery procedures
- Test an upgrade to a new release of Oracle Database
- Test the effect of applications on database performance
- Create a standby database
- Generate reports

Performing Tablespace Point-in-Time Recovery

Identify the situations that require TSPITR

TSPITR stands for Tablespace Point-In-Time Recovery. Recovery Manager TSPITR enables you to recover one or more tablespaces in a database to an earlier time. Unlike incomplete recovery TSPITR can be performed without affecting the rest of the tablespaces and objects in the database. TSPITR is useful in several situations:

- Recovering a logical database to a point different from the rest of the physical database, when multiple logical databases exist in separate tablespaces of one physical database.
- Recovering data lost after data definition language (DDL) operations that change the structure of tables.
- Recovering a table after it has been dropped with the PURGE option.
- Recovering from the logical corruption of a table.
- Recovering dropped tablespaces.

Perform automated TSPITR

RMAN TSPITR is complex enough that I highly recommend reading the "Performing RMAN Tablespace Point-in-Time Recovery (TSPITR)" chapter in the Oracle Database Backup and Recovery User's Guide. While this section will cover the test topic as listed on the Oracle Education site, if you don't really understand TSPITR, you will not have the background to really perform this function. Also, depending on how the questions on this topic are worded in the test, you may not have sufficient context to answer them.

To perform fully automated RMAN TSPITR, the user performing the operation should be able to connect as SYSDBA using operating system authentication. The AUXILIARY DESTINATION parameter is used to set a location for RMAN to use for the auxiliary set data files. The auxiliary destination must be a location on disk with enough space to hold auxiliary set data files.

1. Start an RMAN session on the target database and, if applicable, connect to a recovery catalog.

2. Configure any channels required for TSPITR on the target instance.

3. Run the RECOVER TABLESPACE command, specifying both the UNTIL clause and the AUXILIARY DESTINATION parameter.

```
RECOVER TABLESPACE users, tools
UNTIL LOGSEQ 1700 THREAD 1
AUXILIARY DESTINATION '/u01/auxdest';
```

4. If TSPITR completes successfully, then back up the recovered tablespace before bringing it online. After you perform TSPITR on a tablespace, you can no longer use previous backups of that tablespace.

5. Bring the tablespace back online.

```
RMAN> SQL "ALTER TABLESPACE users, tools ONLINE";
```

Monitoring and Tuning RMAN

Monitoring RMAN sessions and jobs

It is possible to monitor the progress of RMAN backups and restore jobs by querying the V$SESSION_LONGOPS view. V$SESSION_LONGOPS contains detail rows and aggregate rows on RMAN operations. The detail rows are most useful in determining the progress of each backup set.

- **Detail rows** -- These rows describe the files being processed by a single job step. A job step is the creation or restoration of one backup set or data file copy. Detail rows are updated with every buffer that is read or written during the backup step.

- **Aggregate rows** -- These rows describe the files processed by all job steps in an RMAN command. They are updated when each job step completes, so their granularity of update is large.

V$SESSION_LONGOPS Columns Relevant for RMAN

- **SID** -- The server session ID corresponding to an RMAN channel
- **SERIAL#** -- The server session serial number.
- **OPNAME** -- A text description of the row. Examples of details rows include "RMAN: datafile copy", "RMAN: full datafile backup", and "RMAN: full datafile restore". "RMAN: aggregate input" and "RMAN: aggregate output" are the only aggregate rows.
- **CONTEXT** -- For backup output rows, this value is 2. For all other rows except proxy copy (which does not update this column), the value is 1.
- **SOFAR** -- The meaning of this column depends on the type of operation described by this row:
  - ✓ For image copies, the number of blocks that have been read

- ✓ For backup input rows, the number of blocks that have been read from the files being backed up
- ✓ For backup output rows, the number of blocks that have been written to the backup piece
- ✓ For restores, the number of blocks that have been processed to the files that are being restored in this one job step
- ✓ For proxy copies, the number of files that have been copied
- **TOTALWORK** -- The meaning of this column depends on the type of operation described by this row:
  - ✓ For image copies, the total number of blocks in the file.
  - ✓ For backup input rows, the total number of blocks to be read from all files processed in this job step.
  - ✓ For backup output rows, the value is 0 because RMAN does not know how many blocks that it will write into any backup piece.
  - ✓ For restores, the total number of blocks in all files restored in this job step.
  - ✓ For proxy copies, the total number of files to be copied in this job step.

A script designed to query V$SESSION_LONGOPS would be similar to the following:

```
SELECT  sid, serial#, context, sofar, totalwork,
        ROUND(sofar/totalwork*100,2) "%_COMPLETE"
FROM    v$session_longops
WHERE   opname LIKE 'RMAN%'
AND     opname NOT LIKE '%aggregate%'
AND     totalwork != 0
AND     sofar <> totalwork;
```

Tuning RMAN

You can use the DURATION parameter of the BACKUP command to limit the amount of time a given backup job is given to run. To specify a backup duration:

```
BACKUP
DURATION 4:00
TABLESPACE users;
```

The above command will generate an error if the backup does not complete inside the window. If the keyword PARTIAL is specified, RMAN does not report an error but rather displays a message showing which files are not backed up. If the BACKUP command is part of a RUN block, then the remaining commands in the RUN block continue to execute. Specifying FILESPERSET of 1 will save each file as its own backup set. If the window closes before the backup is complete, only the current set (one file) is lost. The following example prevents RMAN from issuing an error and minimizes lost work when a backup partially completes:

```
BACKUP
DURATION 4:00 PARTIAL
TABLESPACE users
FILESPERSET 1;
```

Minimizing Backup Load and Duration

When using DURATION you can run the backup with the maximum possible performance, or run as slowly as possible while still finishing within the allotted time, to minimize the performance impact of backup tasks. To maximize performance, use the MINIMIZE TIME option with DURATION.

```
BACKUP
DURATION 4:00 PARTIAL
MINIMIZE TIME
DATABASE
FILESPERSET 1;
```

When MINIMIZE LOAD is specified, RMAN monitors the progress of the running backup, and periodically estimates how long the backup will take to complete at its present rate. If RMAN estimates that the backup will finish before the end of the backup window, then it slows down the rate of backup so that the full available duration is used. This reduces the overhead on the database associated with the backup. To extend the backup to use the full time available, use the MINIMIZE LOAD option:

```
BACKUP
DURATION 4:00 PARTIAL
MINIMIZE LOAD
DATABASE
FILESPERSET 1;
```

Configure RMAN for Asynchronous I/O

When an RMAN channel accesses a disk for read or write operations, the I/O is either synchronous or asynchronous. When performing synchronous I/O, a server process can perform only one task at a time. When using asynchronous I/O, a server process can begin an I/O operation and then perform some other task while waiting for the I/O to complete. It is also possible to start additional I/O operations without having to wait for the first to complete. When reading from an ASM disk group, you should use asynchronous disk I/O if possible.

Disk I/O Slaves

Many operating systems support asynchronous I/O natively. If an operating system does not support native asynchronous I/O, the database can use special I/O slave processes to simulate it. The availability of disk I/O slaves is controlled by setting the DBWR_IO_SLAVES initialization parameter. By default, the value is 0 and I/O server processes are not used. Set DBWR_IO_SLAVES to enable RMAN to perform asynchronous I/O if and only if your disk does not support asynchronous I/O natively. Any nonzero value for DBWR_IO_SLAVES causes a fixed number of disk I/O slaves to be used for backup and restore, which simulates asynchronous I/O. To enable disk I/O slaves:

1. Start SQL*Plus and connect to the target database.
2. Shut down the database.
3. Set DBWR_IO_SLAVES initialization parameter to a nonzero value.
4. Restart the database.

Tape I/O Slaves

The initialization parameter BACKUP_TAPE_IO_SLAVES specifies whether or not RMAN uses slave processes. Tape devices can only be accessed by a single process at one time, so RMAN uses only the number of slaves necessary for the number of tape devices. If set to true, RMAN will allocate tape buffers from the SGA. When the LARGE_POOL_SIZE initialization parameter is also set, then RMAN allocates buffers from the large pool. When BACKUP_TAPE_IO_SLAVES is set to false, RMAN allocates tape buffers from the PGA. When making use of I/O slaves, set the LARGE_POOL_SIZE initialization parameter to dedicate space for these large memory allocations. This prevents RMAN I/O buffers from competing with the library cache for SGA memory.

Using Flashback Technology

Restore dropped tables from the recycle bin

By default, when a table is dropped, the database does not immediately remove the space associated with the table. Instead, the database renames it and places the table and any associated objects that were dropped in a recycle bin. If it is determined that the table was dropped in error, it can be recovered at a later date. The FLASHBACK TABLE statement is used to restore the table.

The recycle bin is a data dictionary table that contains information required to recover dropped objects. The dropped objects themselves remain where they were before being dropped and still occupy the same amount of disk space. Dropped objects also continue to count against user space quotas until they are explicitly purged or are purged by the database due to tablespace space constraints.

When a tablespace including its contents is dropped, the recycle bin does not come into play. The storage where the objects were does not exist any more. The database purges any entries in the recycle bin for objects that were located in the tablespace. If the recycle bin is disabled, dropped tables and their dependent objects are not placed in the recycle bin; they are just dropped. They must be recovered by other means, such as recovering from backup. The recycle bin is enabled by default.

The FLASHBACK TABLE ... TO BEFORE DROP statement is used to recover objects from the recycle bin. When recovering a table, you must specify either the system-generated name of the table in the recycle bin or the original table name. An optional RENAME TO clause lets you rename the table as you recover it. The USER_RECYCLEBIN view can be used to obtain the system-generated name. To use the FLASHBACK TABLE ... TO BEFORE DROP statement, you need the same privileges required to drop the table.

The following example restores ocp_employees table and assigns to it a new name:

```
FLASHBACK TABLE ocp_employees TO BEFORE DROP
RENAME TO ocp_employees_take2;
```

Perform Flashback Query

Flashback Version Query is used to retrieve metadata and historical data for a specific interval. The interval can be specified by two timestamps or by two SCNs. The metadata returned includes the start and end time a version existed, type of DML operation used to create it, and the identity of the transaction that created each row version. The VERSIONS BETWEEN clause of a SELECT statement is used to generate a Flashback Version Query. The syntax of the VERSIONS BETWEEN clause is: VERSIONS {BETWEEN {SCN | TIMESTAMP} start AND end}.

The pseudocolumns returned by a Flashback version query are:

- **VERSIONS_START[SCN/TIME]** -- Starting System Change Number (SCN) or TIMESTAMP when the row version was created. NULL if version is from before the start value.
- **VERSIONS_END[SCN/TIME]** -- SCN or TIMESTAMP when the row version expired. If NULL, then either the row version was current at the time of the query or the row is for a DELETE operation.
- **VERSIONS_XID** -- Identifier of the transaction that created the row version.
- **VERSIONS_OPERATION** -- Operation performed by the transaction: I for insertion, D for deletion, or U for update. The version is that of the row that was inserted, deleted, or updated.

A given row version is valid starting at VERSIONS_START* up to, but not including, VERSIONS_END*. That is, it is valid for any time 't' such that VERSIONS_START* <= t < VERSIONS_END*. The following three updates were issued against the EMPLOYEES table, with a pause in-between.

```
UPDATE employees SET salary = 97000
WHERE emp_last='McCoy';
UPDATE employees SET salary = 102000
WHERE emp_last='McCoy';
UPDATE employees SET salary = 105000
WHERE emp_last='McCoy';
COMMIT;
```

Then the following Flashback Versions query was run against employees:

```
SELECT versions_starttime, versions_endtime,
       versions_xid, versions_operation AS OP,
       salary
  FROM employees
  VERSIONS BETWEEN TIMESTAMP
      TO_TIMESTAMP('29-MAR-12 11.46.00PM','DD-MON-YY HH:MI:SSAM')
  AND TO_TIMESTAMP('29-MAR-12 11.52.00PM','DD-MON-YY HH:MI:SSAM')
  WHERE emp_last = 'McCoy';
```

```
VERSIONS_STARTTIME    VERSIONS_ENDTIME      VERSIONS_XID      OP SALARY
--------------------  --------------------  ----------------  -- ------
29-MAR-12 11.51.08PM                        09000900A9010000  U  105000
29-MAR-12 11.49.50PM  29-MAR-12 11.51.08PM  04001A003F010000  U  102000
29-MAR-12 11.49.02PM  29-MAR-12 11.49.50PM  03002100A2010000  U   97000
                      29-MAR-12 11.49.02PM                        93500
```

From the results above, you see the three updates against the table, each increasing the salary column value. It's clear when each salary value started and ended (save the initial value for which the start time was outside the window, and the final value which is current (and therefore has no end time). You can use VERSIONS_XID with Oracle Flashback Transaction Query to locate the metadata for any of the three transactions. This will include the SQL required to undo the row change and the user responsible for the change.

Use Flashback Transaction

A Flashback Transaction Query is used to retrieve metadata and historical data for a single transaction or for all transactions in a supplied interval. The data is generated from the static data dictionary view FLASHBACK_TRANSACTION_QUERY. The Flashback Transaction Query creates a column UNDO_SQL. The SQL text in this field is the logical opposite of the DML operation performed by the transaction shown. The code from this field can usually reverse the original transaction within reason (e.g. a SQL_UNDO INSERT operation would be unlikely to insert a row back at the same ROWID from which it was deleted). As a general rule, Oracle Flashback Transaction Query is used in conjunction with an Oracle Flashback Version Query that provides transaction IDs.

```
SELECT operation, start_scn, commit_scn, logon_user
  FROM flashback_transaction_query
    WHERE xid = HEXTORAW('09000900A9010000');

OPERATION    START_SCN COMMIT_SCN LOGON_USER
------------ --------- ---------- ------------
UNKNOWN         393394     393463 OCPGURU
BEGIN           393394     393463 OCPGURU
```

The following statement uses Oracle Flashback Version Query as a subquery to associate each row version with the LOGON_USER responsible for the row data change.

```
SELECT xid, logon_user
  FROM flashback_transaction_query
    WHERE xid IN (
      SELECT versions_xid
      FROM employees VERSIONS BETWEEN TIMESTAMP
        TO_TIMESTAMP('29-MAR-12 11.40.00 PM',
                     'DD-MON-YY HH:MI:SS AM') AND
        TO_TIMESTAMP('29-MAR-12 11.56.00 PM',
                     'DD-MON-YY HH:MI:SS AM')
      );
```

You can use the DBMS_FLASHBACK.TRANSACTION_BACKOUT procedure to roll back a transaction and its dependent transactions while the database remains online. Transaction backout uses undo data to create and execute the compensating transactions to return the affected data to its original state. TRANSACTION_BACKOUT does not commit the DML operations that it performs as part of transaction backout. However, it does hold all the required locks on rows and tables in the right form to prevent other dependencies from entering the system. To make the transaction backout permanent, you must explicitly commit the transaction.

In order to configure a database for the Oracle Flashback Transaction Query feature, the database must be running in ARCHIVELOG mode. In addition, the database administrator must enable supplemental logging.

```
ALTER DATABASE ADD SUPPLEMENTAL LOG DATA;
```

To perform Oracle Flashback Query operations, the administrator must grant appropriate privileges to the user who will be performing them. For Oracle Flashback Query, the administrator can do either of the following:

- To allow access to specific objects during queries, grant FLASHBACK and SELECT privileges on those objects.
- To allow queries on all tables, grant the FLASHBACK ANY TABLE privilege.

For Oracle Flashback Transaction Query, the administrator will need to grant the SELECT ANY TRANSACTION privilege. To allow execution of undo SQL code retrieved by an Oracle Flashback Transaction, the administrator will need to grant: SELECT, UPDATE, DELETE, and INSERT privileges for the appropriate tables. Finally, the administrator will need to grant the user EXECUTE privileges on the DBMS_FLASHBACK Package.

Dependent Transactions

When you are rolling back a given transaction, there may be one or more dependant transactions. A dependent transaction is related by either a write-after-write (WAW) relationship, in which a transaction modifies the same data that was changed by the target transaction, or a Primary Key Constraint relationship, in which a transaction re-inserts the same primary key value that was deleted by the target transaction.

Backout Options

There are four options to TRANSACTION_BACKOUT. The four options determine how the backout operation will handle any transactions that are dependent on the one being backed out:

- **CASCADE** -- Backs out specified transactions and all dependent transactions in reverse-order (children are backed out before parents are backed out).
- **NOCASCADE** -- This is the default option. It assumes there are no dependent transactions. If a dependent transaction exists, it will cause an error.
- **NOCASCADE_FORCE** -- Backs out specified transactions. If there are any dependent transactions, they are ignored. The server executes undo SQL statements for specified transactions in the reverse order of commit times.

- **NONCONFLICT_ONLY** -- Backs out changes to non-conflicting rows of the specified transactions.

Additional Flashback Operations

Perform Flashback Table operations

The Flashback Table feature uses information in the undo tablespace to revert a table to an earlier point in time. When a Flashback Table operation occurs, new rows are deleted and old rows are reinserted.

To use the Flashback Table feature on one or more tables, use the FLASHBACK TABLE SQL statement with a target time or SCN. You need the following privileges to use the Flashback Table feature:

- You must have the FLASHBACK ANY TABLE system privilege or the FLASHBACK object privilege on the table.
- You must have SELECT, INSERT, DELETE, and ALTER privileges on the table.
- To flash back a table to a restore point, you must have the SELECT ANY DICTIONARY or FLASHBACK ANY TABLE system privilege or the SELECT_CATALOG_ROLE role.

For an object to be eligible to be flashed back, the following prerequisites must be met:

- The object must not be included the following categories: tables that are part of a cluster, materialized views, Advanced Queuing (AQ) tables, static data dictionary tables, system tables, remote tables, object tables, nested tables, or individual table partitions or subpartitions.
- The structure of the table must not have been changed between the current time and the target flash back time.
- Row movement must be enabled on the table.
- The undo data in the undo tablespace must extend far enough back in time to satisfy the flashback target time or SCN.

To perform a flashback table operation:

1. Identify the current SCN of the database. This will provide you the information needed to reverse the flashback operation later if you wish.

```
SELECT current_scn
FROM   V$database;
```

2. Identify the time, SCN, or restore point to which you want to return the table.

3. Ensure that enough undo data exists to rewind the table to the specified target.

```
SELECT name, value/60 MINUTES_RETAINED
FROM   v$parameter
WHERE  name = 'undo_retention';
```

4. Ensure that row movement is enabled for all objects that you are rewinding with Flashback Table.

```
ALTER TABLE table_name ENABLE ROW MOVEMENT;
```

5. Determine whether the table that you intend to flash back has dependencies on other tables. If dependencies exist, then decide whether to flash back these tables as well.

6. Execute a FLASHBACK TABLE statement for the objects that you want to flash back. It's possible to flashback to an SCN number or a timestamp value:

```
FLASHBACK TABLE employees
TO SCN 123456;
```

```
FLASHBACK TABLE employees
TO TIMESTAMP TO_TIMESTAMP('2012-05-16 08:30:00', 'YYYY-MM-DD
HH:MI:SS');
```

Configure, Monitor Flashback Database and Perform Flashback Database operations

Oracle's new Flashback Database feature allows you to set the database back to an earlier time in order to correct problems caused by logical data corruption or user errors within a designated time window. Flashback Database is much more efficient than the point-in-time recovery and does not require a backup and restored operation. Flashback Database is accessible through the RMAN command FLASHBACK DATABASE or the SQL statement FLASHBACK DATABASE.

To enable Flashback Database, the database must have Fast Recovery Area. If one exists, you must set a flashback retention target. This target specifies how far in the past it is possible to rewind the database. Flashback Database uses its own logging mechanism, creating flashback logs and storing them in the fast recovery area. The database must be set up in advance to create flashback logs in order to take advantage of this feature. Once configured, at regular intervals, the database copies images of each altered block in every data file into the flashback logs. These block images can later be used to reconstruct the data file contents to any moment for which logs exist. In addition to the flashback logs, redo logs on disk or tape must be available for the entire time period spanned by the flashback logs. The range of SCNs for which there is currently enough flashback log data to support the FLASHBACK DATABASE command is called the flashback database window.

If the fast recovery area does not contain sufficient space for recovery files such as archived redo logs and other backups needed for the retention policy, then the database may delete the flashback logs starting from the earliest SCNs. The flashback retention target does not guarantee that Flashback Database is available for the full period. A larger Fast Recovery Area may be required in this case.

Flashback Database has the following limitations:

- It can only undo changes to a data file made by Oracle Database. It cannot be used to repair media failures, or recover from accidental deletion of data files.
- It cannot undo a shrink data file operation.
- If the database control file is restored from backup or re-created, all accumulated flashback log information is discarded.
- If you Flashback Database to a target time at which a NOLOGGING operation was in progress, block corruption is likely in the database objects and datafiles affected by the NOLOGGING operation.

Normal Restore Points

A normal restore point simply assigns a restore point name to an SCN or specific point in time. It functions as an alias for this SCN. If you use flashback features or point-in-time recovery, the restore point name can be used instead of a time or SCN. Normal restore points eventually age out of the control file if not manually deleted, so they require no ongoing maintenance. The following commands support the use of restore points:

- RECOVER DATABASE and FLASHBACK DATABASE commands in RMAN
- FLASHBACK TABLE statement in SQL

Guaranteed Restore Points

A guaranteed restore point also serves as an alias for an SCN in recovery operations. However, guaranteed restore points never age out of the control file and must be explicitly dropped. It ensures that you can use Flashback Database to rewind a database to the restore point SCN, even if the generation of flashback logs is not enabled. When enabled, a guaranteed restore point enforces the retention of flashback logs all the way back in time to the guaranteed SCN.

Enabling Flashback Database

Ensure the database instance is open or mounted. If the instance is mounted, then the database must be shut down cleanly unless it is a physical standby database.

1. Optionally, set the DB_FLASHBACK_RETENTION_TARGET to the length of the desired flashback window in minutes. The default is 1 day (1440 minutes).

2. Enable the Flashback Database feature for the whole database:

    ```
    ALTER DATABASE FLASHBACK ON;
    ```

3. Optionally, disable flashback logging for specific tablespaces.

Disabling Flashback Database Logging

On a database instances that is either in mount or open state, issue the following command:

```
ALTER DATABASE FLASHBACK OFF;
```

Configuring for Optimal Flashback Database Performance

Maintaining flashback logs does not impose significant overhead on a database instance. Changed blocks are written to the flashback logs at relatively infrequent, regular intervals, to limit processing and I/O overhead. Optimizing performance is primarily a matter of ensuring that the writes occur as fast as possible.

-   Use a fast file system for your fast recovery area, preferably without operating system file caching.
-   Configure enough disk spindles for the file system that holds the fast recovery area.
-   If the storage system used to hold the fast recovery area does not have nonvolatile RAM, then try to configure the file system on striped storage volumes with a relatively small stripe size such as 128 KB.
-   For large databases, set the initialization parameter LOG_BUFFER to at least 8 MB.

Monitoring the Effect of Flashback Database on Performance

There are several database views that allow you to monitor the impact of flashback logs on the database. The V$FLASHBACK_DATABASE_LOG view allows you to monitor the Flashback Database retention target and how much space is being used by the flashback logs in the Fast Recovery Area.

- **OLDEST_FLASHBACK_SCN** -- Lowest system change number (SCN) in the flashback data, for any incarnation
- **OLDEST_FLASHBACK_TIME** -- Time of the lowest SCN in the flashback data, for any incarnation
- **RETENTION_TARGET** -- Target retention time (in minutes)
- **FLASHBACK_SIZE** -- Current size (in bytes) of the flashback data
- **ESTIMATED_FLASHBACK_SIZE** -- Estimated size of flashback data needed for the current target retention

The V$FLASHBACK_DATABASE_STAT view displays statistics for monitoring the I/O overhead of logging flashback data. It also displays the estimated flashback space needed based on previous workloads.

- **BEGIN_TIME** -- Beginning of the time interval
- **END_TIME** -- End of the time interval
- **FLASHBACK_DATA** -- Number of bytes of flashback data written during the interval
- **DB_DATA** -- Number of bytes of database data read and written during the interval
- **REDO_DATA** -- Number of bytes of redo data written during the interval
- **ESTIMATED_FLASHBACK_SIZE** -- Value of ESTIMATED_FLASHBACK_SIZE in V$FLASHBACK_DATABASE_LOG at the end of the time interval.

The V$RECOVERY_FILE_DEST view displays information about the disk quota and current disk usage in the fast recovery area.

- **NAME** -- Location name. This is the value specified in the DB_RECOVERY_FILE_DEST initialization parameter.
- **SPACE_LIMIT** -- Maximum amount of disk space (in bytes) that the database can use for the fast recovery area. This is the value specified in the DB_RECOVERY_FILE_DEST_SIZE initialization parameter.
- **SPACE_USED** -- Amount of disk space (in bytes) used by fast recovery area files created in current and all previous fast recovery areas. Changing fast recovery areas does not reset SPACE_USED to 0.
- **SPACE_RECLAIMABLE** -- Total amount of disk space (in bytes) that can be created by deleting obsolete, redundant, and other low priority files from the fast recovery area
- **NUMBER_OF_FILES** -- Number of files in the fast recovery area

Set up and use a Flashback Data Archive

Oracle 11G's Flashback Data Archive feature allows you to store table-level change history for extended periods of time. It provides the ability to track all transactional changes to a table over its lifetime. The Flashback Data Archive functionality is useful to maintain compliance with record storage policies and audit reports. It's possible to have multiple Flashback Data Archives in a single database, one of which can be (although it's not required), specified as the default for the database. Each Flashback Data Archive in a database is configured with a retention time that determines how long data stored in that particular archive is to be retained.

Flashback archiving is off for any table by default. You can enable flashback archiving for a table if all of the following are true:

- You have the FLASHBACK ARCHIVE object privilege on the Flashback Data Archive that you want to use for that table.
- The table you want to archive is not nested, clustered, temporary, remote, or external.
- The table does not contain LONG or nested columns.

Once flashback archiving is enabled for a table, you can disable it only if you either have the FLASHBACK ARCHIVE ADMINISTER system privilege or you are logged into the database with SYSDBA privileges. While flashback archiving is enabled for a table, some DDL statements are not allowed on it and will generate an ORA-55610 error. Unfortunately from a testing standpoint, many of the disallowed statements under 11g Release 1 are allowed under Release 2.

In 11G Release 1, the disallowed operations are:

- Dropping, renaming, or modifying a column via ALTER_TABLE
- Performing partition or subpartition operations
- Converting a LONG column to a LOB column
- An ALTER TABLE..UPGRADE TABLE operation
- DROP TABLE statement
- RENAME TABLE statement
- TRUNCATE TABLE statement

In 11G Release 2, only the following operations are disallowed:

- ALTER TABLE statement that includes an UPGRADE TABLE clause, with or without an INCLUDING DATA clause
- ALTER TABLE statement that moves or exchanges a partition or subpartition operation
- DROP TABLE statement

Benefits

Flashback Data Archive can be the solution to any number of business requirements. Many government agencies and organizations require that data be kept for a set number of years before being deleted. The settings of a Flashback Data Archive can be specifically configured to meet these requirements. After the specified time period has expired, the data will automatically be aged out of the archive – effectively 'shredding' it without requiring direct intervention. It can help in satisfying some of the storage requirements for such legislative acts as Sarbanes-Oxley and HIPAA. It can provide a source of data for audits. Flashback data archive can also be used as a simple method to recover accidentally altered or deleted data.

Flashback Data Archive Creation and Maintenance

A Flashback Data Archive is created using the CREATE FLASHBACK ARCHIVE statement. If you are logged on with SYSDBA privileges, you can also specify that this is the default Flashback Data Archive for the system. When creating a new flashback data archive, you must specify the following:

- Name of the Flashback Data Archive
- Name of the first tablespace of the Flashback Data Archive
- Retention time (number of days that Flashback Data Archive data for the table is guaranteed to be stored)
- (Optional) Maximum amount of space that the Flashback Data Archive can use in the first tablespace. The default is unlimited.

Create a default Flashback Data Archive named fda1 using a maximum of 15 Gigs of tablespace fda_tbs1. The data will be retained for two years:

```
CREATE FLASHBACK ARCHIVE DEFAULT fda1
TABLESPACE fda_tbs1 QUOTA 15G RETENTION 2 YEAR;
```

Create a Flashback Data Archive named fda2 that uses tablespace fda_tbs2, whose data will be retained for three years:

```
CREATE FLASHBACK ARCHIVE fda2
TABLESPACE fda_tbs2 RETENTION 3 YEAR;
```

Using the ALTER FLASHBACK ARCHIVE statement, you can change the retention time of a Flashback Data Archive; purge some or all of its data; and add, modify, or remove tablespaces. If you are logged on with SYSDBA privileges, you can also make a specific archive the default Flashback Data Archive for the system.

- Make Flashback Data Archive fla1 the default Flashback Data Archive:
  ```
  ALTER FLASHBACK ARCHIVE fda1 SET DEFAULT;
  ```

- Add an additional 5Gigs quota of tablespace fda_tbs1 to Flashback Data Archive fda1:
  ```
  ALTER FLASHBACK ARCHIVE fda1
  ADD TABLESPACE da_tbs1 QUOTA 5G;
  ```

- Add unlimited quota on tablespace fda_tbs3 to Flashback Data Archive fda1:
  ```
  ALTER FLASHBACK ARCHIVE fda1 ADD TABLESPACE tbs3;
  ```

- Change the retention time for Flashback Data Archive fda1 to four years:
  ```
  ALTER FLASHBACK ARCHIVE fda1 MODIFY RETENTION 4 YEAR;
  ```

- Purge all historical data older than one day from Flashback Data Archive fda1:
  ```
  ALTER FLASHBACK ARCHIVE fda1
  PURGE BEFORE TIMESTAMP (SYSTIMESTAMP - INTERVAL '1'
  DAY);
  ```

You can drop a Flashback Data Archive with the DROP FLASHBACK ARCHIVE statement. This statement will delete its historical data, but will not drop the tablespace the archive was stored on. To remove Flashback Data Archive fda1 and all its historical data:

```
DROP FLASHBACK ARCHIVE fda1;
```

Setting Tables to use Flashback Archive

Flashback archiving is disabled for all tables by default. If a flashback data archive exists in the database, and you have the FLASHBACK ARCHIVE privilege on it, you can enable flashback archiving for a table. To enable flashback archiving for a table, you use the FLASHBACK ARCHIVE clause in either a CREATE TABLE or ALTER TABLE statement. It's possible to set the specific Flashback Data Archive where the data for the table will be stored in the FLASHBACK ARCHIVE clause. If no clause is provided, the default Flashback Data Archive for the database will be used. Some examples of making tables use flashback archiving are:

- **Create table dept and use the default Flashback Data Archive:**
```
CREATE TABLE dept (DEPTNO NUMBER(4) NOT NULL,
                   DEPTNAME VARCHAR2(10))
FLASHBACK ARCHIVE;
```

- **Create table employee and use the Flashback Data Archive fda1:**
```
CREATE TABLE dept (DEPTNO NUMBER(4) NOT NULL,
                   DEPTNAME VARCHAR2(10))
FLASHBACK ARCHIVE fda1;
```

- **Enable flashback archiving for the table dept and use the default Flashback Data Archive:**
```
ALTER TABLE dept FLASHBACK ARCHIVE;
```

- **Enable flashback archiving for the table dept and use the Flashback Data Archive fda1:**
```
ALTER TABLE dept FLASHBACK ARCHIVE fda1;
```

- **Disable flashback archiving for the table dept:**
```
ALTER TABLE dept NO FLASHBACK ARCHIVE;
```

Flashback Data Archive Views

The following views in the data dictionary are specific to the Flashback Data Archive:

- DBA_FLASHBACK_ARCHIVE_TABLES
- DBA_FLASHBACK_ARCHIVE
- DBA_FLASHBACK_ARCHIVE_TS

Diagnosing the Database

Set up Automatic Diagnostic Repository

The Automatic Diagnostic Repository (ADR) is a directory structure for diagnostic files such as traces, dumps, the alert log, health monitor reports, and more. The directory structure supports multiple instances and multiple Oracle products. Each instance of each product will store diagnostic data underneath its own home directory within the ADR. ADR provides a unified directory structure along with consistent diagnostic data formats across products and instances. This plus a unified set of tools enables this data to be correlated and analyzed across multiple Oracle products.

DIAGNOSTIC_DEST parameter

Because all diagnostic data, including the alert log, is stored in the ADR, the initialization parameters BACKGROUND_DUMP_DEST and USER_DUMP_DEST have been deprecated. They have been replaced by the initialization parameter DIAGNOSTIC_DEST. The DIAGNOSTIC_DEST parameter identifies the directory which serves as the ADR Base location.

ADR Locations

The V$DIAG_INFO view lists all the important ADR locations for the current Oracle database instance. It also provides the number of active problems and incidents and the tracefiles for the current instance.

- **ADR Base** -- Path of ADR base
- **ADR Home** -- Path of ADR home for the current database instance
- **Diag Trace** -- Location of background process trace files, server process trace files, SQL trace files, and the text-formatted version of the alert log
- **Diag Alert** -- Location of the XML-formatted version of the alert log
- **Default Trace** -- File Path to the trace file for the current session
- **Diag Incident** -- File path for incident packages
- **Diag Cdump** -- Equivalent to cdump. Location for core dump files.
- **Health Monitor** -- Location for health monitor output.

```
SELECT name, value
FROM V$DIAG_INFO;

NAME                    VALUE
--------------------    ------------------------------------------------
Diag Enabled            TRUE
ADR Base                /u01/oracle
ADR Home                /u01/oracle/diag/rdbms/orclbi/orclbi
Diag Trace              /u01/oracle/diag/rdbms/orclbi/orclbi/trace
Diag Alert              /u01/oracle/diag/rdbms/orclbi/orclbi/alert
Diag Incident           /u01/oracle/diag/rdbms/orclbi/orclbi/incident
Diag Cdump              /u01/oracle/diag/rdbms/orclbi/orclbi/cdump
Health Monitor          /u01/oracle/diag/rdbms/orclbi/orclbi/hm
Default Trace File      /u01/oracle/diag/rdbms/orcl/orcl/trace/
                        orcl_ora_224.trc
Active Problem Count     8
Active Incident Count   20
```

Using Support Workbench

Oracle Configuration Manager

The Support Workbench uses Oracle Configuration Manager (OCM) to upload diagnostic data to Oracle Support Services. If Oracle Configuration Manager is not installed or properly configured, the upload may fail. If this happens, a message is displayed with a request that you upload the file manually. You can upload manually through Oracle MetaLink.

Problems vs. Incidents

The fault diagnosability infrastructure in Oracle 11G introduces two concepts for the Oracle Database: problems and incidents. A problem is defined as a critical error in the database. Critical errors manifest as internal errors, such as ORA-00600, ORA-07445, or ORA-04031. Problems are tracked in the ADR using a problem key, which is a text string that describes the problem.

An incident is defined as a single occurrence of a problem. When a problem occurs multiple times, an incident is created for each occurrence. Oracle timestamps the incidents and tracks them in the ADR. Incidents are identified by a numeric incident ID, which is unique within the ADR. Each incident in the database generates the following actions:

- An entry is made in the alert log.
- An incident alert is sent to Oracle Enterprise Manager.
- Diagnostic data about the incident is stored in the form of dump files.

- One or more incident dumps are stored in the ADR in a subdirectory created for that incident.

Flood Control

A single problem could generate hundreds of incidents in a short period of time. If every action generated dumps as described above, this would generate a huge amount of diagnostic data. That much data would not aid diagnosis, would consume significant space in the ADR and could possibly slow down the process of diagnosing and resolving the problem. Oracle applies a flood control mechanism to incident generation to prevent this from happening. After certain thresholds are reached, incidents become flood-controlled. A flood-controlled incident generates an alert log entry and is recorded in the ADR, but does not generate incident dumps.

Threshold levels for incident flood control are predetermined and cannot be changed. They are defined as follows:

- After five incidents occur for the same problem key in one hour, subsequent incidents for this problem key are flood-controlled.
- After 25 incidents occur for the same problem key in one day, subsequent incidents for this problem key are flood-controlled.
- After 50 incidents for the same problem key occur in one hour, or 250 incidents for the same problem key occur in one day, subsequent incidents for the problem key are not recorded at all in the ADR. The database will write a message to the alert log indicating that no further incidents will be recorded.

The Automatic Diagnostic Repository has two distinct retention policies for incidents that determine how long data will be kept on disk from the time of the incident. The incident metadata retention policy determines how long the ADR will retain the metadata on incidents. It defaults to one year. The incident files and dumps retention policy sets the time that dump files will be kept. It is one month by default.

Incident Packaging Service
An incident package is a collection of metadata stored in the Automatic Diagnostic Repository which points to diagnostic data files and other files

both related to a given incident. When creating a package, you select one or more problems to add to the package. The Support Workbench then adds associated problem information, incident information, and diagnostic files to the package. By default only the first and last three incidents for each problem are added to the package. Any incidents that are over 90 days old will not be included. After the package is created, you can add one or more external files, remove selected files, or edit selected files in the package to remove sensitive data. Only the package metadata is modified when performing any of these actions. When you are ready to upload the information to Oracle Support, you create a zip file that contains all the files referenced by the package metadata and upload the zip file through Oracle Configuration Manager. The Incident packaging service (IPS) is the tool which performs all of these steps. Because all diagnostic data in the ADR relating to a critical error are tagged with the incident number, the incident packaging service identifies them automatically and adds them to the zip file.

ADRCI

The Automatic Diagnostic Repository Command Interpreter (ADRCI) is a command-line utility that is part of the Oracle 11G fault diagnosability infrastructure. ADRCI's primary functions include:

- Viewing diagnostic data in the Automatic Diagnostic Repository.
- Viewing Health Monitor reports.
- Packaging incident and problem information for Oracle Support.

Diagnostic data viewable from within ADRCI includes incident and problem descriptions, trace files, dumps, health monitor reports, alert log entries, and more. ADRCI can be used in interactive mode or within scripts. ADRCI can also execute scripts of ADRCI commands just as SQL*Plus can execute scripts of SQL and PL/SQL commands. There is no login to ADRCI -- it is secured by OS-level file permissions only.

ADRCI HOMEPATH

An ADR home is the root directory for all diagnostic data for a particular instance of a given Oracle product or component. All ADR homes share the same hierarchical directory structure that starts at the ADR_BASE directory. Some ADRCI commands can work with multiple ADR homes simultaneously while others require that a single ADR home be set within

ADRCI before issuing the command. The current ADRCI homepath determines the ADR homes that are searched for diagnostic data when an ADRCI command is issued. It does so by pointing to a specific directory within the ADR base hierarchy. When pointed to a single ADR home directory, that ADR home is the only current ADR home. If the homepath points to a higher directory, all ADR homes that are below the directory that is pointed to become current. The ADR homepath is null by default when ADRCI starts, which means that all the ADR homes beneath the ADR_BASE are current. The SHOW HOME and SHOW HOMEPATH commands display the current ADR homes. The SET HOMEPATH command sets the homepath to a specific directory.

Alert Log

Starting with Oracle 11g, the alert log is written as both an XML-formatted file and as a plain text file. You can view either format with any text editor. Alternately, you can use ADRCI to view the XML-formatted alert log with the XML tags stripped. By default, ADRCI displays the alert log in your default editor. You can use the SET EDITOR command to change the editor used by ADRCI.

Trace Files

You can use ADRCI to view the names of trace files that are currently in the ADR. You can view the names of all trace files, or a filtered subset of names. ADRCI has commands to obtain a list of trace files whose file name matches a search string, exist in a particular directory, pertain to a particular incident, or a combination of these. The SHOW TRACEFILE command displays a list of the files in the trace directory and in all incident directories under the current ADR home.

Show Incident

You can use the ADRCI SHOW INCIDENT command to display information about open incidents. For each incident, the incident ID, problem key, and incident creation time are shown. If the ADRCI homepath includes multiple current ADR homes, the report displays incidents from all of them.

```
SHOW INCIDENT

ADR Home =
/u03/app/oracle/product/11.1.0/db_2/log/diag/rdbms/orcl11g/orcl11g:
*********************************************************************
INCIDENT_ID   PROBLEM_KEY      CREATE_TIME
------------- ---------------- -------------------------------------
4218          ORA 603          2011-03-18 21:35:49.322161 -07:00
4219          ORA 600 [4134]   2011-03-20 21:35:47.862114 -07:00
4224          ORA 600 [4138]   2011-04-01 21:35:25.012579 -07:00
3 rows fetched
```

The following are variations on the SHOW INCIDENT command:

```
SHOW INCIDENT -MODE BRIEF
SHOW INCIDENT -MODE DETAIL
SHOW INCIDENT -MODE DETAIL -P "INCIDENT_ID=1681"
```

Packaging Incidents with ADRCI

Packaging incidents is a three-step process:

1. Create a logical incident package.
2. Add diagnostic information to the incident package
3. Generate the physical incident package

You can use either Oracle Enterprise manager or ADRCI to perform incident packaging. Using ADRCI, the initial logical incident package is created with the IPS CREATE PACKAGE command. There are several variants of this command depending on what metadata you want added to the package. For example:

- **IPS CREATE PACKAGE INCIDENT incident_number** will create a package with metadata referencing ADR data for the specified incident number.
- **IPS CREATE PACKAGE PROBLEM problem_ID** will create a package and include diagnostic information for incidents that reference the specified problem ID.
- **IPS CREATE PACKAGE PROBLEMKEY "problem_key"** will create a package with diagnostic information for incidents that reference the specified problem key.
- **IPS CREATE PACKAGE SECONDS sec** will create a package and include diagnostic information for all incidents that occurred from sec seconds ago until now.

- **IPS CREATE PACKAGE** with no additional information will create an empty package. You will need to add all incident data or files manually.

Once a package has been created (empty or not), you can add additional diagnostic information to it. You can add all diagnostic information for a particular incident, or individual named files within the ADR. To add an incident to an existing package, you would use the following command: **IPS ADD INCIDENT incident_number PACKAGE package_number**. To add a file, you would use the command: **IPS ADD FILE filespec PACKAGE package_number**. The file specification must be a fully qualified file name including the path. Only files that are within the ADR base directory hierarchy may be added.

Once the logical package has been created and any additional diagnostic data added, you create a physical package in the form of a zip file. The following commands issued from within ADRCI will generate incident packages:

- **IPS GENERATE PACKAGE package_number IN path** -- This generates a complete physical package in the designated path as a zip file.
- **IPS GENERATE PACKAGE 5 IN /home/george/oracle_support** -- This creates a physical package in the directory /home/george/oracle_support from logical package number 5:
- **IPS GENERATE PACKAGE package_number IN path INCREMENTAL** – This will generate an incremental package. An incremental package will contain only the incidents that have occurred since the last package generation.

Perform Block Media Recovery

Block media recovery allows you to recover individual corrupt data blocks within a data file. Block media recovery is faster than data file media recovery because only blocks needing recovery are restored and recovered. Also, unlike data file media recovery, the affected data files remain online during the recovery process. Prior to the block media recovery capability, a single corrupt block in a datafile required taking the data file offline and restoring from backup.

When the database encounters a corrupt block, it marks the block as media corrupt and then writes it to disk. After being marked corrupt, no subsequent read of the block will be successful until the block is recovered. If block corruption has been detected, block media recovery can be performed manually using the RECOVER ... BLOCK command. By default, RMAN first searches for good blocks in the real-time query physical standby database (if one exists), then flashback logs and then blocks in full or level 0 incremental backups.

All known corrupted block in the database can be located by querying the V$DATABASE_BLOCK_CORRUPTION view. It contains blocks marked corrupt by database components such as RMAN, ANALYZE, dbv, and SQL queries. The following types of corruption result in the addition of rows to this view:

- **Physical corruption** -- Physical corruption, also known as media corruption, means that the database does not recognize the block: the checksum is invalid, the block contains all zeros, or the block header is corrupt. Physical corruption checking is enabled by default. Checksum checking can be disabled by specifying the NOCHECKSUM option of the BACKUP command, but other physical consistency checks cannot be disabled.

- **Logical corruption** -- Logical corruption occurs when the block has a valid checksum, the header and footer match, and so on, but the contents are logically inconsistent. Logical corruption cannot always be corrected by block media recovery. It may be necessary to use alternate recovery methods, such as tablespace point-in-time recovery, or dropping and re-creating the affected objects. Logical corruption checking is disabled by default. It can be enabled by specifying the CHECK LOGICAL option of the BACKUP, RESTORE, RECOVER, and VALIDATE commands.

The following prerequisites apply to the RECOVER ... BLOCK command:

- The target database must run in ARCHIVELOG mode and be open or mounted with a current control file.
- If the target database is a standby database, then it must be in a consistent state, recovery cannot be in session, and the backup must be older than the corrupted file.
- The backups of the data files containing the corrupt blocks must be full or level 0 backups and not proxy copies.
- RMAN can use only archived redo logs for the recovery.
- Flashback Database must be enabled on the target database for RMAN to search the flashback logs for good copies of corrupt blocks.
- The target database must be associated with a real-time query physical standby database for RMAN to search a standby database for good copies of corrupt blocks.

Recovering Individual Blocks

To recover specific data blocks, you must obtain the data file numbers and block numbers of the corrupted blocks. When Oracle encounters a corrupted block, you may get an error in a trace file like the following:

```
ORA-01578: ORACLE data block corrupted (file # 4, block #
213)
ORA-01110: data file 4: '/oracle/oradata/trgt/users01.dbf'
```

To recover this block, perform the following steps:

1. Start RMAN and connect to the target database, which must be mounted or open.

2. Run the SHOW ALL command to confirm that the appropriate channels are preconfigured.

3. Run the RECOVER ... BLOCK command at the RMAN prompt, specifying the file and block numbers for the corrupted blocks.

```
RECOVER
DATAFILE 4 BLOCK 213;
```

Recovering All Blocks in V$DATABASE_BLOCK_CORRUPTION

Rather than recovering blocks individually, you can have RMAN automatically recover all blocks listed in the V$DATABASE_BLOCK_CORRUPTION view. The steps to do this are:

1. Start SQL*Plus and connect to the target database.

2. Query V$DATABASE_BLOCK_CORRUPTION to determine whether corrupt blocks exist.

```
SELECT * FROM V$DATABASE_BLOCK_CORRUPTION;
```

3. Start RMAN and connect to the target database.

4. Recover all blocks marked corrupt in V$DATABASE_BLOCK_CORRUPTION.

```
RMAN> RECOVER CORRUPTION LIST;
```

Once recovered, the blocks will automatically be removed from the view.

Managing Memory

Implement Automatic Memory Management

In Oracle 10G, the then-new parameters sga_target and pga_target automated much of the previously complex task of tuning the SGA and PGA memory areas in a database. Prior to 10G, there were half a dozen parameters to tweak various pools of memory. In Oracle 11G, memory management has gone a step further. The new memory_target parameter is the only value that needs to be set to allow Oracle to automatically manage memory. You need to understand what it does, and how these four parameters relate to each other when set (or not set).

memory_target

When MEMORY_TARGET is set, the database will allocate this much memory on startup, by default granting 60% to the SGA and 40% to the PGA. Over time, as the database runs, it will redistribute memory as needed between the system global area (SGA) and the instance program global area (instance PGA). If MEMORY_TARGET is not set, automatic memory management is not enabled, even if you have set a value for MEMORY_TARGET_MAX.

memory_target_max

When set, this determines the maximum amount of memory that Oracle will grab from the OS for the SGA and PGA. If this value is not set, it will default to the MEMORY_TARGET value.

sga_target

This value is not required if using automatic memory management. If this value is set and MEMORY_TARGET is also set, then the value of SGA_TARGET becomes the <u>minimum</u> amount of memory allocated to the SGA by automatic memory management.

pga_aggregate_target

This value is not required if using automatic memory management. If this value is set and MEMORY_TARGET is also set, then the value of PGA_AGGREGATE_TARGET becomes the <u>minimum</u> amount of memory allocated to the PGA by automatic memory management.

Manually configure SGA parameters

Manual shared memory management is enabled by disabling both automatic memory management and automatic shared memory management. If both the MEMORY_TARGET initialization parameter and the SGA_TARGET initialization parameter are set to 0, you must then set values for the various SGA components.

Buffer Cache

The buffer cache initialization parameters determine the size of the buffer cache component of the SGA. As a rule, larger cache sizes reduce the number of disk reads and writes. If the database contains multiple block sizes, you must have the DB_CACHE_SIZE and at least one DB_nK_CACHE_SIZE parameter set. The sizes and numbers of nonstandard block size buffers are specified by the following parameters:

DB_2K_CACHE_SIZE
DB_4K_CACHE_SIZE
DB_8K_CACHE_SIZE
DB_16K_CACHE_SIZE
DB_32K_CACHE_SIZE

Multiple Buffer Pools

The database buffer cache can be configured with separate buffer pools that either keep data in the buffer cache or make the buffers available for new data immediately after using the data blocks. Individual schema objects (tables, clusters, indexes, and partitions) can then be assigned to one of the buffer pools to control how their data blocks age out of the cache. The buffer pools are:

- **KEEP** -- Retains the schema object's data blocks in memory and is defined with the DB_KEEP_CACHE_SIZE parameter.
- **RECYCLE** -- Eliminates data blocks from memory as soon as they are no longer needed and is defined with the DB_RECYCLE_CACHE_SIZE parameter.
- **DEFAULT** -- Contains data blocks from schema objects that are not assigned to any buffer pool or are explicitly assigned to the DEFAULT pool.

Shared Pool Size

The SHARED_POOL_SIZE initialization parameter is a dynamic parameter that lets you specify or adjust the size of the shared pool component of the SGA. Beginning with Oracle Database 10g R1, the internal SGA overhead is included in the user-specified value of SHARED_POOL_SIZE. When setting this parameter you must include the internal SGA overhead in addition to the desired value for shared pool size.

Large Pool Size

The LARGE_POOL_SIZE initialization parameter lets you specify or adjust the size of the large pool component of the SGA. The large pool is an optional component and will not exist if the LARGE_POOL_SIZE parameter is omitted.

Java Pool Size

The JAVA_POOL_SIZE initialization parameter lets you specify or adjust the size of the java pool component of the SGA. Oracle selects an appropriate default value if this is not set explicitly.

Streams Pool Size

The STREAMS_POOL_SIZE initialization parameter lets you specify or adjust the size of the Streams Pool component of the SGA. If set to 0, then the Oracle Streams product transfers memory from the buffer cache to the Streams Pool when needed.

Result Cache Maximum Size

The RESULT_CACHE_MAX_SIZE initialization parameter enables you to specify the maximum size of the result cache component of the SGA. The default maximum size is chosen by the database based on total memory available to the SGA and on the memory management method currently in use.

Configure automatic PGA memory management

In 11G, Oracle automatically manages the total amount of memory allocated to the instance PGA. It is possible to control this amount with the initialization parameter PGA_AGGREGATE_TARGET. Once set, Oracle attempts to keep the total amount of PGA memory allocated across all database server processes and background processes from exceeding this target.

When using automatic PGA memory management, SQL work areas for all dedicated server sessions are sized automatically. Any *_AREA_SIZE initialization parameters will be ignored for these sessions. There are several dynamic performance views that provide PGA memory use statistics. Statistics on allocation and use of work area memory is available in the following dynamic performance views:

V$SYSSTAT
V$SESSTAT
V$PGASTAT
V$SQL_WORKAREA
V$SQL_WORKAREA_ACTIVE

The following three columns in the V$PROCESS view report the PGA memory allocated and used by an Oracle Database process:

PGA_USED_MEM
PGA_ALLOCATED_MEM
PGA_MAX_MEM

Managing Database Performance

Use the SQL Tuning Advisor

As SQL statements are executed by the Oracle database, the query optimizer works to generate good execution plans for them. The query optimizer has two modes of operation: a normal mode and a tuning mode.

- **Normal mode** -- The optimizer compiles the SQL and generates an execution plan with sub-second time constraints during which it must find a good execution plan.
- **Tuning mode** -- The optimizer performs additional analysis to check whether the 'normal' execution plan can be improved upon. The output of the query optimizer in tuning mode is not an execution plan, but a series of actions, along with a rationale and expected benefit for producing a significantly superior plan.

When running in the tuning mode, the optimizer is referred to as the Automatic Tuning Optimizer. While running in tuning mode, the optimizer can take several minutes to tune a single statement. It's not practical to invoke the Automatic Tuning Optimizer every time a query has to be hard-parsed. It is meant to be used for complex and high-load SQL statements that have a negative impact on the database. The Automatic Tuning Optimizer performs four types of tuning analysis.

Statistics Analysis

Oracle's query optimizer makes use of object statistics to generate execution plans. When statistics are stale or missing, the optimizer can generate sub-optimal execution plans. The Automatic Tuning Optimizer checks for missing or stale statistics, and produces two types of output. The first is recommendations to gather statistics for objects where the statistics are stale or missing. The second type of statistics output is auxiliary information. This takes the form of statistics for objects with no statistics, and statistic adjustment factor for objects with stale statistics. This auxiliary information is stored in an object called a SQL Profile.

SQL Profiling

Sometimes the query optimizer produces inaccurate estimates about an attribute of a statement due to lack of information, leading to poor execution plans. This can sometimes be corrected by manually adding hints to the SQL in order to guide the optimizer into making better decisions. Hints are not always effective, are labor intensive, and are often impractical when using packaged applications. SQL profiling is intended to be a solution for this problem. The Automatic Tuning Optimizer stores additional data regarding the SQL statement called a SQL Profile. The profile consists of auxiliary statistics specific to that statement. A SQL Profile collects additional information using sampling and partial execution techniques to help the optimizer make decisions about cardinality and other traits of the SQL query. In addition, the Automatic Tuning Optimizer also uses execution history information of the SQL statement to appropriately set optimizer parameter settings in the profile. An accepted SQL Profile is stored persistently in the data dictionary. SQL Profiles are specific to the particular query they were created for. After accepting the profile, if that statement is executed in the database again, the optimizer uses normal statistics in addition to the profile data when generating an execution plan. The additional information makes it possible to produce well-tuned plans for the corresponding SQL statement without. A SQL Profile does not act like a stored outline to freeze the execution plan of a SQL statement. As changes happen to the tables against which the SQL is run, the execution plan can change with the same SQL Profile.

Access Path Analysis

The use of indexes can tremendously enhance performance of a SQL statement. Properly used, they can reduce the need for full table scans on large tables and speed up join operations when querying multiple tables. Adding indexes to tables is a common method to drop query times. One of the functions of the optimizer is to investigate whether a new index can significantly enhance the performance of a query. If it identifies the need for such an index, it recommends its creation. The Automatic Tuning Optimizer does not analyze how its index recommendation can affect the remainder of the SQL workload. It therefore also recommends running the SQL Access Advisor utility on the SQL statement along with a representative SQL workload. Unlike the Automatic Tuning Optimizer, the

SQL Access Advisor does look at the impact of creating an index on the entire SQL workload before making any recommendations.

SQL Structure Analysis

The Automatic Tuning Optimizer identifies common problems with the structure of SQL statements that can lead to poor performance. The structure issues could be syntactic, semantic, or design problems with the statement. Whatever the issue, Automatic Tuning Optimizer makes relevant suggestions to restructure the SQL statements. It will suggest an alternative that is similar, but not equivalent, to the original statement. For example, the optimizer may suggest replacing a UNION operator with a UNION ALL or to replace NOT IN with NOT EXISTS. The developer can then decide if the advice is applicable in the given situation. SQL structure changes require a deep understanding of the data properties and should be implemented only after considering all the implications.

Automatic SQL Tuning

The Automatic Tuning Optimizer runs as an automated task on high-load SQL statements identified by the AWR as tuning candidates. This task, called Automatic SQL Tuning, runs in the default maintenance windows on a nightly basis. By default, it will run for at most one hour during any given maintenance window and perform the following steps:

1. Identify SQL candidates in the AWR for tuning. Oracle uses data from the AWR to generate a list of potential SQL statements that are eligible for tuning. Candidates will typically be repeating high-load statements that have a significant impact on the system. Only statements that have an execution plan with a high potential for improvement will be marked for tuning. Recursive SQL and statements that have been tuned recently are ignored, as are parallel queries, DMLs, AND DDLs. The candidates are then ordered based on their performance impact. The performance impact of a SQL statement is calculated by summing the CPU time and the I/O times captured in the AWR for that SQL statement in the past week.
2. Each SQL statement is individually tuned by calling the SQL Tuning Advisor. During the tuning process, all recommendation types are considered and reported, but only SQL profiles can be implemented automatically.

3.   Test SQL profiles by executing the SQL statement. If a SQL profile is recommended, the tuning advisor will execute the SQL statement with and without the profile.

4.   Optionally implement the SQL profiles. Only if the performance improves at least threefold will the SQL profile be accepted automatically (and then only if the ACCEPT_SQL_PROFILES task parameter is set to TRUE). A profile will not be implemented if the objects referenced in the SQL statement have stale optimizer statistics. SQL profiles that have been implemented automatically will have their type set to AUTO in the DBA_SQL_PROFILES view.

Use the SQL Access Advisor to tune a workload

Whereas SQL Tuning Advisor is designed to make sure that SQL statements are taking the most efficient path to provide the data requested, SQL Access Advisor is designed to help make sure that an efficient path to the data exists. SQL Access advisor offers recommendations intended to achieve the proper set of materialized views, materialized view logs, and indexes for a given workload. As a general rule, as the number of materialized views and indexes increase, query performance improves. SQL Access Advisor weighs trade-offs between space usage and query performance. SQL Access Advisor makes recommendations, each of which will contain one or more actions. If a recommendation contains multiple actions, all of the individual actions must be implemented to achieve the full benefit. If the Advisor decides that one or more base tables should be partitioned, it will collect all individual partition actions into a single recommendation. In that case, note that some or all of the remaining recommendations might be dependent on implementing the partitioning recommendation. It's not possible to view index and materialized view advice in isolation of the underlying table's partitioning.

Modes of Operation

SQL Access Advisor has two modes of operation: problem solving and evaluation. The default mode is problem solving. In this mode, SQL Access Advisor will attempt to solve access method problems by looking for new objects to create. When operating in evaluation mode, SQL Access Advisor will only comment on existing access paths that the given workload will use. A problem solving run might recommend creating a new index whereas an evaluation only scenario will only produce recommendations such as retaining an existing index. The evaluation mode is useful in determining which indexes and materialized views are actually being used by a given workload.

Intermediate Results

With 11G, SQL Access Advisor allows you to see intermediate results during the analysis operation. Previously, results were unavailable until the processing had completed or was interrupted by the user. With the change, it is possible to access results in the recommendation and action tables while the SQL Access Advisor task is still executing. Intermediate results represent recommendations only for the portion of the workload that has been executed up to that point in time. If the entire workload must be evaluated, then you should allow the task to complete normally. Recommendations made by the advisor early in the evaluation process will not have any base table partitioning recommendations. Partitioning analysis requires most of the workload to be processed before it's clear whether partitioning would be beneficial.

Creating Tasks

You create advisor tasks to define what it is you want to analyze and where the analysis results should be placed. It's possible to create any number of tasks, each with a given specialization. All are based on the same Advisor task model and share the same repository. Tasks are created using the CREATE_TASK procedure:

```
VARIABLE task_id NUMBER;
VARIABLE task_name VARCHAR2(255);
EXECUTE :task_name := 'MYTASK';
EXECUTE DBMS_ADVISOR.CREATE_TASK
        ('SQL Access Advisor', :task_id, :task_name);
```

SQL Tuning Sets

The input workload for the SQL Access Advisor is the SQL Tuning Set. An important benefit of using a SQL Tuning Set is that because SQL Tuning Sets are stored as separate entities, they can be referenced by many Advisor tasks. A workload reference will be removed when a parent Advisor task is deleted or when the workload reference is removed from the Advisor task by the user. A SQL Tuning Set workload is created using DBMS_SQLTUNE. You can pull SQL Workload objects into a SQL Tuning Set using DBMS_ADVISOR:

```
EXECUTE
DBMS_ADVISOR.COPY_SQLWKLD_TO_STS('MYWORKLOAD','MYSTS','NEW');
```

Linking Tasks and Workloads

Tasks must be linked to a SQL Tuning Set in order to generate advisor recommendations. You create links with the ADD_STS_REF procedure, using their respective names to link the task to a Tuning Set. Once a connection has been defined, the SQL Tuning Set is protected from removal or update.

```
EXECUTE DBMS_ADVISOR.ADD_STS_REF('MYTASK', null,
'MYWORKLOAD');
```

Removing a Link

Before a task or a SQL Tuning Set workload can be deleted, any existing links between the task and the workload must be removed. Links are removed using the DELETE_STS_REF procedure.

```
EXECUTE DBMS_ADVISOR.DELETE_STS_REF('MYTASK', null,
'MYWORKLOAD');
```

Recommendation Options

Parameters for a given task must be defined using the SET_TASK_PARAMETER procedure before recommendations can be generated. If parameters are not defined, then the defaults are used. You can set task parameters by using the SET_TASK_PARAMETER procedure.

```
DBMS_ADVISOR.SET_TASK_PARAMETER (
      task_name IN VARCHAR2,
      parameter IN VARCHAR2,
      value IN [VARCHAR2 | NUMBER]);
```

Generating Recommendations

You can generate recommendations by using the EXECUTE_TASK procedure. After it completes, the DBA_ADVISOR_LOG table will show execution status and the number of recommendations and actions produced. EXECUTE_TASK is a synchronous operation, so control will not be returned to the user until the operation has completed, or is interrupted. Upon completion, you can check the DBA_ADVISOR_LOG table for the execution status. The recommendations can be queried by task name in DBA_ADVISOR_RECOMMENDATIONS and the actions in DBA_ADVISOR_ACTIONS.

```
EXECUTE DBMS_ADVISOR.EXECUTE_TASK('MYTASK');
```

Understand Database Replay

Before making significant hardware or software upgrades to a production Oracle database, typically extensive testing is performed to verify the changes will not adversely affect the system. However, making such testing close enough to reality to provide a valid test is very difficult. Often problems are encountered after the upgrade that were not located during the testing period. There are various third-party tools on the market to provide load testing for Oracle, simulating the workload from multiple users. However, the workloads generated are not as complex and interactive as that generated by a real production system. Oracle 11G's new Database Replay feature enables system administrators to perform real-world testing by capturing the production database workload and replaying it on another database. In addition, it provides analysis and reporting of potential problems and recommend ways to resolve these problems.

What is captured by Database Replay

Oracle Database Replay captures all external database calls made to the system during the workload capture period. The capture includes all relevant information about the client request, such as SQL text, bind values, and transaction information. Background activities of the database and scheduler jobs are not captured. In addition, the following types of client requests are not captured in a workload:

- Direct path load of data from external files using utilities such as SQL*Loader
- Shared server requests (Oracle MTS)
- Oracle Streams
- Advanced replication streams
- Non-PL/SQL based Advanced Queuing (AQ)
- Flashback queries
- Oracle Call Interface (OCI) based object navigations
- Non SQL-based object access
- Distributed transactions

Using Workload capture and replay

It is a best practice to restart the database before capturing the production workload. This ensures that ongoing and dependent transactions are allowed to be completed or rolled back before the capture begins. If the database is not restarted before the capture, transactions that are in progress or have yet to be committed will be only partially captured in the workload.

Define Workload Filters

By default, all activities from all user sessions are recorded during workload capture. Workload filters can be used to include or exclude specific user sessions during the workload capture. You can use either inclusion filters or exclusion filters in a workload capture, but not both simultaneously. Inclusion filters specify user sessions that will be captured in the workload. Exclusion filters enable you to specify user sessions that will not be captured in the workload. To add filters to a workload capture, you use the DBMS_WORKLOAD_CAPTURE.ADD_FILTER procedure. To remove an existing filter, you use the DBMS_WORKLOAD_CAPTURE.DELETE_FILTER procedure.

Setting Up the Capture Directory

Before starting the workload capture, you must decide on the directory where the captured workload will be stored. Before starting the capture, verify that the directory is empty and has enough space for the workload. If the directory runs out of disk space during a workload capture, the capture will stop.

Starting a Workload Capture

You should have a well-defined starting point for the workload so that the database being used to replay the workload can be restored to the same point before starting the captured workload. It is best not to have any active user sessions when starting a workload capture. Active sessions may have ongoing transactions which will not be replayed completely. Consider restarting the database in RESTRICTED mode prior to starting the workload capture. When the workload capture begins, the database will automatically switch to UNRESTRICTED mode and normal operations can continue while the workload is being captured. You begin a workload capture using the procedure DBMS_WORKLOAD_CAPTURE.START_CAPTURE.

Stopping a Workload Capture

To stop a workload capture in progress, you use the FINISH_CAPTURE procedure of the DBMS_WORKLOAD_CAPTURE package.

Exporting AWR Data for Workload Capture

You can export AWR data from the production machine in order to enable detailed analysis of the workload on both systems. This data is required if you plan to run the AWR Compare Period report on a pair of workload captures or replays. To export AWR data, you use the DBMS_WORKLOAD_CAPTURE.EXPORT_AWR procedure.

Workload Capture Views

The following views allow you to monitor a workload capture. You can also use Oracle Enterprise Manager to monitor a workload capture:

- **DBA_WORKLOAD_CAPTURES** -- Lists all the workload captures that have been created in the current database.
- **DBA_WORKLOAD_FILTERS** -- Lists all workload filters used for workload captures defined in the current database.

Preparing the Replay

After the workload has been captured, it's necessary to preprocess the capture files prior to using them in a replay. Preprocessing converts the captured data into replay files and creates the required metadata needed to replay the workload. After preprocessing the captured workload, it can be replayed multiple times on any replay system running the same version of Oracle. As a general rule, it's recommended to move the capture files to another system for preprocessing. While the capture itself has a minimal overhead, workload preprocessing can be time consuming and resource intensive. It is better that this step be performed on the test system where the workload will be replayed rather than on the production database. Capture files are processed using the PROCESS_CAPTURE procedure of the DBMS_WORKLOAD_REPLAY package.

Replaying the Workload

After you have preprocessed a captured workload, it can be replayed on the test system. In the workload replay, Oracle will perform the actions recorded during the workload capture. It will re-create all captured external client requests with the same timing, concurrency, and transaction dependencies that occurred on the production system. Database Replay uses a program called the replay client to re-create the external client requests. You may need to use multiple replay clients depending on the scope of the captured workload. The replay client has an imbedded calibration tool to help determine the number of replay clients required for a given workload. The entire workload from the production database is replayed. This includes DML and SQL queries, so the data in the replay system must be as logically similar to the data in the capture system as possible. Ensuring the systems are as identical as possible will minimize data divergence and enable a more reliable analysis of the replay. Replaying a database workload requires the following steps:

Setting Up the Replay Directory

The captured workload must have been preprocessed and copied to the replay system. An Oracle directory object for the directory to which the preprocessed workload has been copied must exist in the replay system.

Resolving References to External Systems

A captured workload may contain references to external systems, such as database links or external tables. These should be reconfigured to avoid impacting production systems during replay. External references that need to be resolved before replaying a workload include: Database links, external tables, directory objects, URLs, and e-mail addresses. If these external connections are not changed before starting the replay, you could end up changing data in production systems, sending emails to users, and other undesirable actions.

Remapping Connections

Connection strings used to connect to the production system are captured in the workload. You must remap these connection strings to the replay system for the replay to succeed. The clients can then connect to the replay system using the remapped connections. For Oracle Real Application Cluster databases, you can map all connection strings to a load balancing connection string.

Specifying Replay Options

There are several options that determine the behavior of the database replay.

- **synchronization** -- determines whether the COMMIT order will be preserved during replay. By default, synchronization is enabled. All transactions will be executed only after all dependent transactions have been committed. If you disable this option, the replay will likely have significant data divergence. This may be not be a problem if the workload consists primarily of independent transactions. Not preserving the commit order can also lead to a faster replay, if 'stress testing' of the replay system is desirable.
- **connect_time_scale** -- enables you to scale the elapsed time between the time when the sessions connected to the database during the workload capture began and when each session connects during the replay. This option allows you to manipulate the session connect time during replay with a given percentage value. By default, the value is 100, which will attempt to connect all sessions as captured. Setting this parameter to 0 will attempt to connect all sessions immediately.
- **think_time_scale** -- allows you to scale user think time during replay. User think time is the elapsed time while the replayed user waits between issuing calls within a single session. A value of 100 means that time between calls will be the same as they were during the capture. A value of zero will eliminate all wait time between calls.
- **think_time_auto_correct** -- If user calls are being executed slower during replay than during capture, you can make the database replay attempt to catch up by setting this parameter to TRUE. When set to true, it will make the replay client shorten the think time between calls, so that the overall elapsed time of the replay will more closely match the captured elapsed time.

Setting Up Replay Clients

The replay client is a multithreaded program where each thread submits a workload from a captured session. It is an executable file named wrc located in the $ORACLE_HOME/bin directory. The replay user that wrc logs in as needs the DBA role and cannot be SYS. The wrc executable uses the following syntax:

```
wrc [user/pword[@server]] MODE=[value] [keyword=[value]]
```

The mode parameter specifies the action to be taken when the wrc executable is run. Possible values include replay (the default), calibrate, and list_hosts. The parameter keyword specifies the options to use for the execution and is dependent on the mode selected. To display the possible keywords and their corresponding values, run the wrc executable without any arguments. The modes that you can select when running the wrc executable and their corresponding keywords are:

- **replay (the default)** -- runs a captured workload. In replay mode, the wrc executable accepts the following keywords:
  - ✓ **userid and password** -- specify the user ID and password of a replay user for the replay client. If unspecified, the user ID defaults to the SYSTEM user.
  - ✓ **server** -- specifies the connection string that is used to connect to the replay system. If unspecified, the value defaults to an empty string.
  - ✓ **replaydir** -- specifies the directory that contains the preprocessed workload capture you want to replay. If unspecified, it defaults to the current directory.
  - ✓ **debug** -- specifies whether debug data will be created.
  - ✓ **workdir** -- specifies the directory where the client logs will be written. This parameter is only used in conjunction with the debug parameter.
  - ✓ **connection_override** -- specifies whether to override the connection mappings stored in the DBA_WORKLOAD_CONNECTION_MAP view.
- **calibrate** -- causes wrc to return an estimate of the number of replay clients and hosts that are required to replay a particular workload. In calibration mode, wrc accepts the following keywords:
  - ✓ **replaydir** -- specifies the directory that contains the preprocessed workload capture. It defaults to the current directory.
  - ✓ **process_per_cpu** -- specifies the maximum number of client processes that can run per CPU. The default value is 4.

- ✓ **threads_per_process** -- specifies the maximum number of threads that can run within a client process. The default value is 50.
- **list_hosts** -- Displays the hosts that participated in a workload capture and workload replay. In list_hosts mode, the wrc executable accepts only one keyword:
  - ✓ replaydir -- specifies the directory that contains the preprocessed workload capture you want to replay. If unspecified, it defaults to the current directory

Analysis and Reporting

Once the workload replay has completed, in-depth reporting is available so that you can perform detailed analysis of both the workload capture and the replay operation. The summary report provides basic information such as errors encountered during replay and data divergence in rows returned by DML or SQL queries. A comparison of several statistics between the source and replay servers is also provided. You can use Automatic Workload Repository reports for advanced analysis of the workload processing between the two servers.

Space Management

Manage resumable space allocation

Resumable space allocation allows for large database operations to be suspended and later resumed in the event of a space allocation failure. Prior to this feature, when such an operation ran out of space, it immediately failed and was rolled back. Even with the new capability, a statement executes in a resumable mode only if its session has been enabled for resumable space allocation.

If a resumable statement is suspended, the error causing the suspension is reported in the alert log, and the system issues the Resumable Session Suspended alert. If the user has a trigger on the AFTER SUSPEND system event, it will be executed. If the error condition is resolved before the timeout period expires, the suspended statement resumes automatically and the Resumable Session Suspended alert is cleared. If a statement is suspended for the full timeout interval (the default is two hours), it will wake up and return the exception to the user. It is possible for a resumable statement to be suspended and resumed multiple times during execution.

There are three classes of correctable errors:

- Out of space
- Maximum extents reached
- Space quota exceeded

Enabling and Disabling Resumable Space Allocation

Resumable space allocation is only possible if the session a statement is executed in has resumable mode enabled. Resumable mode can be enabled at the system level with the RESUMABLE_TIMEOUT initialization parameter, or users can enable it at the session level using the ALTER

SESSION statement. Users can only do this if they have been granted the RESUMABLE system privilege.

By default, the RESUMABLE_TIMEOUT parameter is set to 0. This disables resumable for all sessions by default. Providing a non-zero value will enable resumable space allocation by default for all sessions with the supplied number of seconds. The parameter can be changed dynamically by issuing an ALTER SYSTEM SET RESUMABLE_TIMEOUT command with the desired value. Within a session, a user can alter the resumable behavior with the ALTER SESSION SET RESUMABLE_TIMEOUT statement.

A user can enable or disable resumable mode for a session with ALTER SESSION:

```
ALTER SESSION ENABLE RESUMABLE;
ALTER SESSION DISABLE RESUMABLE;
```

When resumable mode is enabled for a session, the following statement specifies that resumable transactions will time out and error after 3600 seconds:

```
ALTER SESSION ENABLE RESUMABLE TIMEOUT 3600;
```

When enabling resumable statements, it is possible to give them a name. If a name is not set, a statement name will default to 'User username(userid), Session sessionid, Instance instanceid'.

```
ALTER SESSION ENABLE RESUMABLE TIMEOUT 3600 NAME 'Really Huge
Table Insert';
```

The following views can be queried to obtain information about the status of resumable statements:

- **DBA_RESUMABLE & USER_RESUMABLE** -- Contain rows for all currently executing or suspended resumable statements. They can be used to monitor the progress of, or obtain specific information about, resumable statements.

- **V$SESSION_WAIT** -- When a statement is suspended the session invoking the statement is put into a wait state. A row is inserted into this view for the session with the EVENT column containing "statement suspended, wait error to be cleared".

The DBMS_RESUMABLE package helps control resumable space allocation. The following procedures can be invoked:

- **ABORT(sessionID)** -- This procedure aborts a suspended resumable statement.
- **GET_SESSION_TIMEOUT(sessionID)** -- This function returns the current timeout value of resumable space allocation for the session with sessionID.
- **SET_SESSION_TIMEOUT(sessionID, timeout)** -- This procedure sets the timeout interval of resumable space allocation for the session with sessionID.
- **GET_TIMEOUT()** -- This function returns the current timeout value of resumable space allocation for the current session.
- **SET_TIMEOUT(timeout)** -- This procedure sets a timeout value for resumable space allocation for the current session.

Describe the concepts of transportable tablespaces and databases

The Transportable Tablespaces feature enables you to copy a tablespace from one Oracle database to another. The tablespace can be locally or dictionary managed and is does not have to be the same block size as the destination database standard block size. Moving data using transportable tablespaces is much faster than either an export/import or unload/load of the same data. This is because the datafiles are copied to the destination location, and Data Pump is used just to transfer the metadata for the objects it contains to the new database.

There are two ways to transport a tablespace:

- Issuing manual commands via SQL*Plus, RMAN, and Data Pump.
- Using the Transport Tablespaces Wizard in Enterprise Manager

It is possible to transport tablespaces across platforms. Not all platforms are supported for cross-platform transport. You can determine if an OS is supported by querying the V$TRANSPORTABLE_PLATFORM view. This view also indicates each platform's endian format (byte ordering). If the source and destination platforms are of different endianness, then an additional step is required to convert the tablespace being transported. The following query displays the platforms that support cross-platform tablespace transport:

```
SELECT platform_id PID, platform_name, endian_format
FROM   v$transportable_platform
WHERE  platform_name LIKE '%Linux%'
ORDER BY platform_name;

PID  PLATFORM_NAME        ENDIAN_FORMAT
---- -------------------- -------------
10   Linux IA (32-bit)    Little
11   Linux IA (64-bit)    Little
13   Linux x86 64-bit     Little
```

Before a tablespace can be transported to a different platform, the datafile header must identify the platform to which it belongs. In an Oracle Database with compatibility set to 10.0.0 or later, you can accomplish this by making the datafile read/write at least once.

The following limitations apply to transporting tablespaces:

- The source and the destination databases must use compatible database character sets.
- The destination database cannot contain a tablespace of the same name. If it does, you must rename either the tablespace to be transported or the one in the destination database.
- Objects with underlying objects (such as materialized views) or contained objects (such as partitioned tables) are not transportable unless all of the underlying or contained objects are in the tablespace being transported.

- Encrypted tablespaces have several conditions (See the Admin Guide for more details).
- Tablespaces that do not use block encryption but that contain tables with encrypted columns cannot be transported.

Steps to Transport a Tablespace

Task 1: Determine if Platforms are Supported and Determine Endianness

This task is only required if the source and destination platforms are different. If both platforms are supported, you can perform the transport. However, if they do not have the same endianness, you must perform a conversion of the tablespace set either at the source or destination database. To determine of the platforms are supported and their endianness, query the V$TRANSPORTABLE_PLATFORM view.

Task 2: Pick a Self-Contained Set of Tablespaces

It is only possible to transport a set of tablespaces that has no references from inside the set of tablespaces pointing outside of the tablespaces. An example of a violation to this rule would be an index inside the set of tablespaces that is for a table outside of the set. You can call the TRANSPORT_SET_CHECK procedure in the package DBMS_TTS to check if a tablespace is self-contained. The following statement can be used to determine whether tablespace ocpts is self-contained, with referential integrity constraints taken into consideration (indicated by TRUE).

```
EXECUTE DBMS_TTS.TRANSPORT_SET_CHECK('ocpts', TRUE);
```

Any violations will be visible in the TRANSPORT_SET_VIOLATIONS view. If the set of tablespaces is self-contained, this view is empty. Violations must be resolved before the tablespace can be transported.

Task 3: Generate a Transportable Tablespace Set

1. Start SQL*Plus and connect to the database as an administrator or as a user who has either the ALTER TABLESPACE or MANAGE TABLESPACE system privilege.
2. Make all tablespaces in the set read-only.
3. Invoke the Data Pump export utility as user system and specify the tablespaces in the transportable set.
4. Check the log file for errors
5. When finished, exit back to SQL*Plus:

If the tablespace is being transported to a platform with a different endianness, you can convert it before transporting the tablespace set. To convert the datafiles, you will use the RMAN CONVERT TABLESPACE command.

Task 4: Transport the Tablespace Set

Complete the following steps:

1. Transport both the datafiles and the export (dump) file of the tablespaces the destination database.
2. If you are transporting the tablespace set to a platform with a different endianness than the source platform, and have not yet converted the tablespace set, do so now with the RMAN CONVERT TABLESPACE command.

Task 5: (Optional) Restore Tablespaces to Read/Write Mode

Make the transported tablespaces read/write again at the source database.

Task 6: Import the Tablespace Set

Any privileged user can perform this task. To import a tablespace set, complete the following steps:

1. Import the tablespace metadata using the Data Pump Import utility, impdp:
2. If required, put the tablespaces into read/write mode on the destination database.

Reclaim wasted space from tables and indexes by using the segment shrink functionality

The online segment shrink capability of Oracle allows you to reclaim fragmented free space below the high watermark in a segment. Shrinking a segment provides the following benefits:

*   Compaction of data leads to better cache utilization.
*   Compacted data requires fewer blocks to be scanned in full table scans.

Segment shrink is an online, in-place operation that does not interfere with DML operations or queries. Concurrent DML operations are blocked for a short time at the end of the shrink operation, when the space is deallocated. Indexes are maintained during the shrink operation and remain usable after completion. No extra disk space needs to be allocated. Segment shrink reclaims unused space both above and below the high water mark. By default, a shrink operation compacts the segment, adjusts the high water mark, and releases the reclaimed space.

Segment shrink requires that rows be moved to new locations. You must first enable row movement in the object and disable any rowid-based triggers. Shrink operations can be performed only on segments in locally managed tablespaces with automatic segment space management (ASSM). Within an ASSM tablespace, all segment types are eligible for online segment shrink except the following:

- IOT mapping tables
- Tables with rowid based materialized views
- Tables with function-based indexes
- SECUREFILE LOBs
- Compressed tables

Invoking Online Segment Shrink

You can shrink space in a table, index-organized table, index, partition, subpartition, materialized view, or materialized view log. You do this using ALTER TABLE, ALTER INDEX, ALTER MATERIALIZED VIEW, or ALTER MATERIALIZED VIEW LOG statement with the SHRINK SPACE clause. There are two optional clauses that control the behavior of the shrink operation:

- **COMPACT** – This clause divides the shrink segment operation into two phases. When specified, the Database defragments the segment space and compacts the table rows but does not reset the high water mark or deallocate space. You can reissue the SHRINK SPACE clause without the COMPACT clause during off-peak hours to complete the shrink operation.
- **CASCADE** – This clause extends the segment shrink operation to all dependent segments of the object.

Examples

Shrink a table and all of its dependent segments:

```
ALTER TABLE employees SHRINK SPACE CASCADE;
```

Shrink a single partition of a partitioned table:

```
ALTER TABLE customers MODIFY PARTITION cust_P1 SHRINK SPACE;
```

Managing Resources

Understand the database resource manager

The Oracle Database Resource Manager (DRM) is designed to optimize resource allocation among concurrent database sessions. It attempts to prevent problems that can happen if the operating system makes resource decisions when presented with high overhead without having awareness of the database needs. DRM helps to overcome these problems by giving the database more control over how hardware resources are allocated. DRM enables you to classify sessions into groups based on session attributes, and then allocate resources to those groups in a way that optimizes hardware utilization for your application environment. The information that performs the functions of classifying sessions and assigning resources is called a resource plan. Oracle 11G comes with sophisticated new built-in resource plans for DRM. There is a mixed-workload plan that provides resource management for a mixed environment consisting of both OLTP and DSS/batch jobs. There is a Data Warehouse plan that provides resource management for a data warehousing environment. Finally there is the maintenance plan that provides resource management for the maintenance window. These plans are shipped with Oracle 11G and provide resource management directives that should provide immediate benefits for the majority of database installations. There are three elements of DRM:

- **Resource consumer group**: A group of sessions that are grouped together based on resource requirements.
- **Resource plan**: A container for directives that specify how resources are allocated to resource consumer groups.
- **Resource plan directive**: Associates a resource consumer group with a particular plan and specifies how resources are to be allocated to that resource consumer group.

Resource Plan Directives

A resource plan directive for a consumer group, can specify limits for CPU and I/O resource consumption for sessions in that group. This is done by specifying the action to be taken if a call within a session exceeds one of the specified limits. These actions, called switches, occur only for sessions that are running and consuming resources, not waiting for user input or for CPU cycles. The possible actions are the following:

- The session is switched to a consumer group with lower resource allocations.
- The session is killed (terminated).
- The session's current SQL statement is aborted.

The resource plan directive attribute that determines which of the above three actions will be taken is SWITCH_GROUP. This attribute specifies the consumer group to which a session is switched if the specified criteria are met. If the value of this parameter is a consumer group, the session will be switched to that group. If the group name is 'CANCEL_SQL', the current call for that session is canceled. Finally, if the group name is 'KILL_SESSION', then the session is killed.

Per session I/O or CPU Limits
The resource plan directive attributes that can be used in specifying the criteria to use in making switch determinations follow. If not set, all default to UNLIMITED.

- **SWITCH_TIME**: Specifies the time (in CPU seconds) that a call can execute before an action is taken.
- **SWITCH_IO_MEGABYTES**: Specifies the number of megabytes of I/O that a session can transfer (read and write) before being switched.
- **SWITCH_IO_REQS**: Specifies the number of I/O requests that a session can execute before an action is taken.

Be sure you understand the meaning of and difference between the two criteria for the test.

SWITCH_ESTIMATE and SWITCH_FOR_CALL
These two resource plan attributes can be used to modify the behavior of resource plan switching:
- **SWITCH_ESTIMATE**: If TRUE, the database estimates the execution time of each call. If the estimated execution time exceeds SWITCH_TIME, the session is moved to the SWITCH_GROUP before beginning the call. The default is FALSE.

SWITCH_FOR_CALL: If TRUE, a session that was automatically switched to another consumer group is returned to its original consumer group when the top level call completes. The default is NULL.

Create and use Database Resource Manager Components

It's possible to create some very complex resource plans with Database Resource Manager. The full capabilities of DRM are beyond the scope of the exam (and this guide). The example presented is a plan that is complex enough to familiarize you with a number of the DRM calls. In this example, session mapping rules start all sessions in the START_HERE group. If a query takes more than 10 minutes of CPU time, it is switched to a consumer group with a maximum utilization limit of 15%. This limits the amount of resources that they can consume until a DBA intervenes.

```
BEGIN
  DBMS_RESOURCE_MANAGER.CREATE_PENDING_AREA();

  DBMS_RESOURCE_MANAGER.CREATE_CONSUMER_GROUP (
      CONSUMER_GROUP => 'START_HERE',
      COMMENT        => 'Sessions start here');

  DBMS_RESOURCE_MANAGER.CREATE_CONSUMER_GROUP (
      CONSUMER_GROUP => 'BAD_SQL_NO_BISCUIT',
      COMMENT        => 'Sessions switched here to punish bad
SQL');

  DBMS_RESOURCE_MANAGER.CREATE_PLAN(
    PLAN    => 'No_Biscuit',
    COMMENT => 'Find bad queries. Swat bad queries.');

  DBMS_RESOURCE_MANAGER.CREATE_PLAN_DIRECTIVE(
    PLAN                  => 'No_Biscuit',
    GROUP_OR_SUBPLAN      => 'START_HERE',
    COMMENT               => 'Max CPU 10 minutes before
switch',
    MGMT_P1               => 75,
    switch_group          => 'BAD_SQL_NO_BISCUIT',
    switch_time           => 600);

  DBMS_RESOURCE_MANAGER.CREATE_PLAN_DIRECTIVE(
    PLAN                  => 'No_Biscuit',
    GROUP_OR_SUBPLAN      => 'OTHER_GROUPS',
```

```
    COMMENT                 => 'Mandatory',
    MGMT_P1                 => 25);

  DBMS_RESOURCE_MANAGER.CREATE_PLAN_DIRECTIVE(
    PLAN                    => 'No_Biscuit',
    GROUP_OR_SUBPLAN        => 'BAD_SQL_NO_BISCUIT',
    COMMENT                 => 'Limited CPU',
    MGMT_P2                 => 100,
    MAX_UTILIZATION_LIMIT   => 15);

  DBMS_RESOURCE_MANAGER.VALIDATE_PENDING_AREA();
  DBMS_RESOURCE_MANAGER.SUBMIT_PENDING_AREA();
END;
/
```

Automating Tasks with the Scheduler

Create a job, program, and schedule

The Oracle Scheduler is implemented by the procedures and functions in the DBMS_SCHEDULER package. The Scheduler enables you to control when and where various tasks occur. The Scheduler provides sophisticated, flexible enterprise scheduling functionality, which you can use to:

- **Run database program units** -- You can run PL/SQL anonymous blocks, PL/SQL stored procedures, and Java stored procedures on the local database or on remote Oracle databases.
- **Run external executables** -- You can run applications, shell scripts, and batch files, on the local system or on one or more remote systems.
- **Schedule job execution using multiple methods** -- The scheduled can employ time-based scheduling, event-based scheduling, and dependency scheduling.
- **Prioritize jobs based on business requirements** -- The Scheduler provides control over resource allocation among competing jobs.
- **Manage and monitor jobs** -- You can track information such as the status of the job and the last run time of the job by querying views using Enterprise Manager or SQL.
- **Execute and manage jobs in a clustered environment** -- The Scheduler fully supports execution of jobs in a Real Application Cluster environment.

To use the Scheduler, you create Scheduler objects. Schema objects define the what, when, and where for job scheduling. Scheduler objects enable a modular approach to managing tasks. One advantage of the modular approach is that objects can be reused when creating new tasks that are similar to existing tasks.

The principal Scheduler object is the job. A job defines the action to perform, the schedule for the action, and the location or locations where the action takes place. Most other scheduler objects are created to support jobs.

Some key points about the Oracle Scheduler:

- You may run PL/SQL and Java stored procedure, C functions, regular SQL scripts, and UNIX or Windows scripts.
- You can create time-based or event-based jobs. Events can be application-generated, scheduler-generated, or generated by a file watcher.
- The Scheduler consists of the concepts: Program, Job, Schedule, Job class, Resource group, Window and Window Group.
- The Scheduler architecture consists primarily of the job table, job coordinator, and the job workers (or slaves).

There are multiple elements of the Scheduler architecture. All except jobs are optional.

- **Programs** -- The scheduler allows you to optionally create programs which hold metadata about a task, but no schedule information. A program may relate to a PL/SQL block, a stored procedure or an OS executable file. Programs are created using the CREATE_PROGRAM procedure.
- **Schedules** -- Schedules optionally define the start time, end time and interval related to a job.
- **Jobs** -- Jobs can either be made up of predefined parts (programs and schedules) or completely self contained depending on which overload of the CREATE_JOB procedure is used to create them.
- **Job Classes** -- Job classes allow grouping of jobs with similar characteristics and resource requirements which eases administration.

- **Windows** -- Windows provide the link between the scheduler and the resource manager, allowing different resource plans to be activated at different times.
- **Window Groups** -- A window group is a collection of related windows.

Creating Jobs

```
DBMS_SCHEDULER.CREATE_JOB(
    JOB_NAME        => 'TEST_JOB1',
    JOB_TYPE        => 'PLSQL_BLOCK',
    JOB_ACTION      => 'BEGIN mytestproc; END;',
    START_DATE      => SYSTIMESTAMP,
    REPEAT_INTERVAL => 'FREQ=DAILY;INTERVAL=2',
    END_DATE        => NULL,
    COMMENTS        => 'TEST JOB')
```

- **JOB_TYPE** -- Possible values are: plsql_block, stored_procedure, executable
- **JOB_ACTION** -- Specifies the exact procedure, command, or script that the job will execute.
- **START_DATE and END_DATE** -- Specify the date that a new job should start and end. (Many jobs may not have an end_date parameter)
- **REPEAT_INTERVAL** -- You can specify a repeat interval using a PL/SQL date/time expression or a database calendaring expression.
- **COMMENTS** -- Allows you to add descriptive text to the job.

Enabling and Disabling Jobs

All jobs are disabled by default when you create them. You must explicitly enable them in order to activate and schedule them. The following examples show how to enable and disable a job.

```
DBMS_SCHEDULER.ENABLE ('TEST_JOB1')

DBMS_SCHEDULER.DISABLE ('TEST_JOB1')
```

Creating a Program

A program describes what is to be run by the Scheduler and is a separate entity from a job. A job runs at a certain time or because a certain event occurred, and calls a program. Different jobs can use the same program and run the program at different times and with different settings.

```
DBMS_SCHEDULER.CREATE_PROGRAM(
  PROGRAM_NAME    => 'UPDATE_STATS',
  PROGRAM_ACTION  => 'OCPUSER.UPDATE_SCHEMA_STATS',
  PROGRAM_TYPE    => 'STORED_PROCEDURE',
  ENABLED         => TRUE)
```

Once a program exists, it a job can be created using the program component as follows:

```
DBMS_SCHEDULER.CREATE_JOB(
JOB_NAME         => 'TEST_JOB1',
PROGRAM_NAME     => 'UPDATE_STATS',
REPEAT_INTERVAL=> 'FREQ=DAILY;BYHOUR=03',
ENABLED          => TRUE)
```

Creating a Schedule

A schedule object specifies when and how many times a job is run. Schedules can be shared by multiple jobs. When you create a schedule, Oracle provides access to PUBLIC. Thus, all users can use your schedule, without any explicit grant of privileges to do so. You specify the start and end times using the TIMESTAMP WITH TIME ZONE data type. The Scheduler also supports all NLS_TIMESTAMP_TZ_FORMAT settings. You must use a calendaring expression to create the repeat interval.

```
DBMS_SCHEDULER.CREATE_SCHEDULE(
   SCHEDULE_NAME    => 'SCHEDULE_12HR',
   START_DATE       => SYSTIMESTAMP,
   END_DATE         => NULL,
   REPEAT_INTERVAL  => 'FREQ=HOURLY;INTERVAL= 12',
   COMMENTS         => 'EVERY 12 HOURS')


DBMS_SCHEDULER.CREATE_JOB(
   JOB_NAME      => 'TEST_JOB02',
   PROGRAM_NAME  => 'UPDATE_STATS',
   SCHEDULE_NAME => 'SCHEDULE_12HR')
```

Creating a Window

Windows link the scheduler to the resource manager, allowing different resource plans to be activated at different times. Since job classes point to resource consumer groups, and therefore resource plans, this mechanism allows control over the resources allocated to job classes and their jobs during specific time periods.

```
DBMS_SCHEDULER.create_window (
   window_name      => 'test_window_1',
   resource_plan    => NULL,
   schedule_name    => 'SCHEDULE_12HR',
   duration         => INTERVAL '60' MINUTE,
   window_priority  => 'LOW',
   comments         => 'Window with a predefined schedule.');
```

Use a time-based or event-based schedule for executing Scheduler jobs

Time-Based Schedules

The DBMS_SCHEDULER.CREATE_SCHEDULE procedure allows you to define a repeating time period on which a job should be executed. Named schedules thus created can then be referenced by multiple jobs.

```
BEGIN
  DBMS_SCHEDULER.CREATE_SCHEDULE(
    schedule_name      =>   'bimonthly_15th',
    start_date         =>   SYSTIMESTAMP,
    repeat_interval    =>
'FREQ=MONTHLY;INTERVAL=2;BYMONTHDAY=15;BYHOUR=9,17;);
END;
/


BEGIN
  DBMS_SCHEDULER.CREATE_JOB (
    job_name            =>   'BIMONTHLY_ALL_HANDS',
    program_name        =>   'BIG_TIME_WASTER',
    schedule_name       =>   'BIMONTHLY_15TH'
    enabled             =>   TRUE,
    comments            =>   'my event-based job');
END;
/
```

The Scheduler job BIMONTHLY_ALL_HANDS will be executed every second month, on the 15th, at 9AM and 5PM.

Event-Based Schedules

An event is a message sent by one application or system process to another to indicate that some action or occurrence has been detected. There are three kinds of events consumed by the Scheduler:

- **Events raised by your application** -- An application can raise an event to be consumed by the Scheduler, which reacts by starting a job. For example, when an employee has been terminated, it can raise an event that starts a job to suspend the employee's access to critical systems.
- **File arrival events raised by a file watcher** -- You can create a file watcher to watch for the arrival of a file on a system. You can then configure a job to start when the file watcher detects the presence of the file.

- **Scheduler-generated events** -- The Scheduler can raise an event to indicate state changes that occur within the Scheduler itself. For example, the Scheduler can raise an event when a job starts, when a job completes, when a job stalls, and so on.

You can create a schedule that is based on an event. The schedule can then be used for multiple jobs. To do so, use the CREATE_EVENT_SCHEDULE procedure, or use Enterprise Manager. The following is an example of creating an event schedule:

```
BEGIN
  DBMS_SCHEDULER.CREATE_EVENT_SCHEDULE (
    schedule_name      =>  'EMP_TERM_EVENT_SCHEDULE',
    start_date         =>  SYSTIMESTAMP,
    event_condition    =>  'tab.employees.event_type =
''TERMINATION''',
    queue_spec         =>  'emp_events_q, emp_agent');
END;
/
```

```
BEGIN
  DBMS_SCHEDULER.CREATE_JOB (
    job_name      =>  'TERM_JOB',
    program_name  =>  'SUSPEND_ACCOUNT_ACCESS',
    schedule_name =>  'EMP_TERM_EVENT_SCHEDULE'
    enabled       =>  TRUE,
    comments      =>  'my event-based job');
END;
/
```

The Scheduler job TERM_JOB will now run whenever the TERMINATION event is raised.

Create lightweight jobs
Lightweight Jobs

New with Oracle 11G is the concept of lightweight jobs. In comparison with traditional DBMS_SCHEDULER jobs, lightweight jobs have lower creation overhead and generate less redo. You'd use lightweight jobs when you have a large number of short-duration jobs that run frequently. Lightweight jobs have the following characteristics:

- Unlike regular jobs, they are not schema objects.
- They have a significant improvement in create and drop time over regular jobs because they do not have the overhead of creating a schema object.
- They have lower average session creation time than regular jobs.
- They have a small footprint on disk for job metadata and runtime data.

Lightweight jobs can only be generated via a job template. You create a lightweight job by using the job_style attribute 'LIGHTWEIGHT' while creating the template. The alternative job_style is 'REGULAR', which is the default. Like programs and schedules, regular jobs are schema objects. A regular job offers more flexibility but entails more overhead when it is created or dropped. A lightweight job must reference a program object to specify a job action. The program must be enabled when the lightweight job is created, and the program type must be either 'PLSQL_BLOCK' or 'STORED_PROCEDURE'. You cannot grant privileges on lightweight jobs. They inherit privileges from the specified program. A user with privileges on the program being called has corresponding privileges on the lightweight job.

Use job chains to perform a series of related tasks

A DBMS_SCHEDULER chain is a named series of tasks that are linked together to achieve a combined objective. Chains allow you to implement dependency based scheduling. Jobs in a chain will be started depending on the outcomes of one or more previous jobs. The basic steps to create and use a chain are:

1. Create a chain object
2. Define the steps in the chain
3. Add rules

4. Enable the chain
5. Create a job that points to the chain

Creating the Chain

You create a chain by using the CREATE_CHAIN procedure.

```
BEGIN
  DBMS_SCHEDULER.CREATE_CHAIN (
      chain_name          => 'ocp_chain',
      rule_set_name       => NULL,
      evaluation_interval => NULL,
      comments            => 'Working on the chain gang');
END;
/
```

Adding Chain Steps

Once a chain object has been created, you must define one or more chain steps. Each step can point to one of the following:

- A Scheduler program object (program)
- Another chain (a nested chain)
- An event schedule or inline event

```
BEGIN
  DBMS_SCHEDULER.DEFINE_CHAIN_STEP (
      chain_name      =>  'ocp_chain1',
      step_name       =>  'ocp_step1',
      program_name    =>  'ocp_program1');
  DBMS_SCHEDULER.DEFINE_CHAIN_STEP (
      chain_name      =>  'ocp_chain1',
      step_name       =>  'ocp_step2',
      program_name    =>  'ocp_chain2');
END;
/
```

The program or chain used in the step does not have to exist during definition. It must exist and be enabled when the chain runs, or an error will be generated.

The DEFINE_CHAIN_EVENT_STEP procedure allows you to create steps that wait on events. Procedure arguments can point to an event schedule or can include an inline queue specification and event condition.

```
BEGIN
DBMS_SCHEDULER.DEFINE_CHAIN_EVENT_STEP (
    chain_name             =>   'ocp_chain1',
    step_name              =>   'ocp_step3',
    event_schedule_name    =>   'ocp_event_schedule');
END;
/
```

Adding Rules to a Chain

The DEFINE_CHAIN_RULE procedure enables you to add a rule to a chain. Chain rules define when steps are run and define dependencies between steps. Each rule has a condition and an action. If a rule's condition evaluates to TRUE, its action is performed. Conditions are usually based on the outcome of one or more previous steps. Scheduler chain condition syntax takes one of the following two forms:

```
stepname [NOT] {SUCCEEDED|FAILED|STOPPED|COMPLETED}
stepname ERROR_CODE {comparision_operator|[NOT] IN}
{integer|list_of_integers}
```

Starting and Ending the Chain

At least one rule must have a condition that always evaluates to TRUE so that the chain can start when the chain job starts. At least one chain rule must contain an action of 'END'. The following example defines a rule that starts the chain at step **step1** and a rule that starts step **step2** when **step1** completes.

```
BEGIN
DBMS_SCHEDULER.DEFINE_CHAIN_RULE (
    chain_name    =>    'ocp_chain1',
    condition     =>    'TRUE',
    action        =>    'START step1',
    rule_name     =>    'ocp_rule1',
    comments      =>    'start the chain');
```

```
DBMS_SCHEDULER.DEFINE_CHAIN_RULE (
    chain_name    =>   'ocp_chain1',
    condition     =>   'step1 completed',
    action        =>   'START step2',
    rule_name     =>   'ocp_rule2');
END;
/
```

Setting an Evaluation Interval for Chain Rules

Chain rules are evaluated at the start of the chain job and at the end of each chain step. it is also possible to configure a chain to have its rules evaluated at a repeating time interval, such as once per hour.

```
BEGIN
DBMS_SCHEDULER.CREATE_CHAIN (
    chain_name          => 'ocp_chain1',
    rule_set_name       => NULL,
    evaluation_interval => INTERVAL '30' MINUTE,
    comments            => 'Chain with 30 minute evaluation
interval');
END;
/
```

Enabling Chains

A chain must be enabled before it can be run by a job.

```
BEGIN
DBMS_SCHEDULER.ENABLE ('ocp_chain1');
END;
/
```

Creating Jobs for Chains

A chain can be initiated by the RUN_CHAIN procedure or by creating and scheduling a job of type 'CHAIN'.

```
BEGIN
DBMS_SCHEDULER.CREATE_JOB (
    job_name        => 'chain_job_1',
    job_type        => 'CHAIN',
    job_action      => 'ocp_chain1',
    repeat_interval =>
'freq=daily;byhour=4;byminute=0;bysecond=0',
    enabled         => TRUE);
END;
/
```

Running Chains

You can use the RUN_CHAIN procedure to run a chain without having to first create a chain job for the chain.

```
BEGIN
DBMS_SCHEDULER.RUN_CHAIN (
    chain_name    =>  'ocp_chain1',
    job_name      =>  'ocp_chain_job');
END;
/
```

Administering the Scheduler

Create Windows and Job Classes

DBMS_SCHEDULER job windows link the scheduler to the Data Resource Manager. This allows different resource plans to be activated at different times. When used in conjunction with job classes (that point to resource consumer groups), windows provides control over the resources allocated to job classes during specific time periods. Only one window can be active (open) at any time, with one resource plan assigned to the window. The affect of resource plan switches is instantly visible to running jobs which are assigned to job classes. The following statement creates a window called finance_window in SYS:

```
BEGIN
  DBMS_SCHEDULER.CREATE_WINDOW (
      window_name          => 'finance_window',
      schedule_name        => 'fin_schedule',
      resource_plan        => 'fin_resourceplan',
      duration             => interval '60' minute,
      comments             => 'Finance window');
END;
/
```

Job classes allow jobs with similar characteristics to be grouped together in order to simplify administration of resource requirements. When the JOB_CLASS parameter of the CREATE_JOB procedure is left undefined, the job is assigned to the DEFAULT_JOB_CLASS. To create a job class, you use the CREATE_JOB_CLASS procedure. The following statement creates a job class called finance_jobs in SYS that uses a service called accounting and is assigned to the resource consumer group finance_group.

```
BEGIN
  DBMS_SCHEDULER.CREATE_JOB_CLASS (
    job_class_name               =>  'finance_jobs',
    resource_consumer_group      =>  'finance_group',
    service                      =>  'accounting',
    comments                     =>  'All finance jobs');
END;
/
```

Use advanced Scheduler concepts to prioritize jobs

Advanced scheduler features, such as windows, window groups, and job classes in conjunction with the Data Resource Manager, allow you to create a robust system of job schedules that will automatically adjust resource usage to fit your needs. Jobs that consume significant resources can be made to run when database usage is low. High priority jobs can be made to kick off earlier or be allocated additional resources.

Schedule Windows

The priority of any given job is not static and can change depending on when it is run. During business hours, jobs supporting application processes would have a high priority, while evenings might allocate more resources to data loads, backup operations and database maintenance processes such as refreshing materialized views. The mechanism to support resource allocation of this type is Scheduler Windows. Every window can be assigned a priority. If windows overlap, the one with the highest priority is chosen over the others because only one can be active at any given time.

Scheduler windows work in tandem with job classes to control database resource allocation. A given window specifies the resource plan that should be activated when the window opens. Job classes in turn map to a resource consumer group or to a database service, which can map to a consumer group. Any job running during a window will be granted resources based on the consumer group of its job class and the resource plan of the window. Windows have three key attributes:

- **Schedule** -- When the window is in effect.
- **Duration** -- How long the window is open.
- **Resource plan** -- The resource plan that activates when the window opens.

The following statement creates a window with low priority for jobs that should be run in the early morning hours (1AM to 5AM) on weekdays.

```
BEGIN
    DBMS_SCHEDULER.CREATE_WINDOW (
        window_name        => 'wee_hours',
        resource_plan      => 'maintenance_workload_plan',
        start_date         => '28-JAN-13 01.00.00 AM',
        repeat_interval    => 'freq=daily;
byday=mon,tue,wed,thu,fri',
        duration           => interval '4' hour,
        window_priority    => 'low');
END;
/
```

Prioritizing Jobs Within a Window

When a database has a significant number of jobs -- some will be more critical than others. Assigning a priority level to jobs helps to ensure that the automatic execution of jobs fulfils your business requirements. When several jobs are to be run in a given window, each will have a set priority (which may be the default). Jobs can be given a priority at either the job or the job class level.

- Class-level prioritization is performed using resource plans.
- Job-level prioritization via the job priority attribute determines start times.

The overall priority of a given job is determined first by the resource consumer group that the job's job class is assigned to and the current resource plan. Within the job class, you can assign priority values of 1-5 to individual jobs. If two jobs in the same job class are scheduled to start at the same time, the higher priority job will take precedence. If two jobs have the same assigned priority value, the job with the earlier start date takes precedence. When no priority is assigned to a job, it defaults to 3. The following statement changes the job priority for **ocp_job** to a setting of 2:

```
BEGIN
  DBMS_SCHEDULER.SET_ATTRIBUTE (
    name            =>   'ocp_job',
    attribute       =>   'job_priority',
    value           =>   2);
END;
/
```

The priority of individual jobs does not transfer across job classes. If two jobs running in a given window are in different job classes, prioritization is not guaranteed. A high-priority job in one class might be started after a lower-priority job in another.

ABOUT THE AUTHOR

Matthew Morris is an Oracle Database Administrator and Developer currently employed as a Database Engineer with Computer Sciences Corporation. Matthew has worked with the Oracle database since 1996 when he worked in the RDBMS support team for Oracle Support Services. Employed with Oracle for over eleven years in support and development positions, Matthew was an early adopter of the Oracle Certified Professional program. He was one of the first one hundred Oracle Certified Database Administrators (version 7.3) and in the first hundred to become an Oracle Certified Forms Developer. In the years since, he has upgraded his Database Administrator certification for releases 8i, 9i, 10G and 11G, and added the Application Express Expert certification. Outside of Oracle, he has CompTIA certifications in Linux+ and Security+.

www.ingramcontent.com/pod-product-compliance
Lightning Source LLC
Chambersburg PA
CBHW071152050326
40689CB00011B/2084